20° W

Grímsey

Melrakka-
slétta

Þistilfjörður

Langanes

Fagranes

Finnafjörður

Digranes

Tjörnes

Axar-
fjörður

SIGLUFJÖRÐUR

ÓLAFSFJÖRÐUR

Eyjafjörður

HÚSAVÍK

Ásbyrgi

Vopnafjörður

Heraðsflói

Skagafjörður

Hólar

AKUREYRI

Goðafoss

Laxá

Dettifoss

Krafla

Jökulsá á Fjöllum

Dyrfjöll

SAUÐÁRKRÓKUR

Námaskarð

Hverfjall

Mývatn

Héraðsvötn

Blanda

Herðubreið

Egilsstaðir

SEYÐISFJÖRÐUR

NESKAUPSTAÐUR

Lagarfljót

Eskifjörður

65°

Ódáða hraun

Dyngjufjöll

Askja

Drekagil

Skjálfandafljót

Sprengisandur

Skeiðarárlón

Jökulsá á Brú

Snæfell

Austfirðir

Hvera-
vellir

Hofsjökull

Trölladyngja

Kverkjökull

kull

Arnarfell
hið mikla

Dyngjujökull

Brúarjökull

Langjökull

Karlsdráttur

Kjölur

Kverkfjöll

Hvítárvatn

Kerlingar
fjöll

Þjórsá

Bárðarbunga

Jarlhettur

VATNAJÖKULL

Hauka-
lur

Gullfoss

Koldukvísl

Grímsvötn

Grímsfjall

Háabunga

Breiðabunga

Þórisvatn

Jökul-
heimar

Tungnaár-
jökull

Pálsfjall

Esjufjall

Höfn

Vesturhorn

Þjórsá

Suðursveit

Hornafjörður

holt

Búrfell

Tungnaá

Skaftárjökull

Grænalón

Máfabyggðir

Breiðamerkurjökull

Hekla

Eldgjá

Skaftá

Lakagígar

Eggjar

Skeiðarárjökull

Hvannadals
hnjúkur

Jökulsá á Breiðamerkursandi

Næfurholt

Landmanna-
laugar

Hverfisfljót

Lómagnúpur

Skeiðará

Öræfajökull

Torfajökull

Skeiðarársandur

Markarfljót

Þórsmörk

Skaftá

Eldhraun

Mýrdals-
jökull

Eyjafjalla-
jökull

Katla

Mýrdalssandur

VESTMANNAEYJAR

Vík
í Mýrdal

20° V

0 10 20 30 40 50 60 70 80 km

0   10   20   30   40   50 miles

D1346583

ice and fire

ice and fire

contrasts of Icelandic nature
text and pictures by
Hjálmar R. Bárðarson

PUBLISHED BY HJÁLMAR R. BÁRÐARSON, REYKJAVÍK

SOME POINTS ON THE PRONUNCIATION OF ICELANDIC LETTERS

Most Icelandic place names and personal names in this book appear in their Icelandic form. Of the special Icelandic letters the following might be mentioned: Ð, ð is a voiced consonant pronounced like the th in English weather, Þ, þ is a voiceless consonant, pronounced like the th in English thin. Æ, æ is a diphthong, pronounced like the i in English like. Ö, ö has a sound that somewhat resembles the English vowel sound in bird. Á, á resembles the diphthong in English house. Ó, ó somewhat resembles the diphthong in English home. Ú, ú resembles the vowel sound in English too, and Í, í resembles the vowel sound in English feel. É, é is pronounced like the English semi-vowel in yes. It should be noted, however, that in some of these cases there are only rough approximations.

Translation: Sölvi Eysteinsson M. A.

THIRD ENGLISH EDITION:

PUBLISHER:
HJÁLMAR R. BÁRÐARSON,
P.O. BOX 998, REYKJAVIK, ICELAND.

FIRST EDITION 1971,
SECOND EDITION 1973,
THIRD EDITION 1980.

PRINTED IN THE NETHERLANDS BY
JOH. ENSCHEDÉ EN ZONEN
GRAFISCHE INRICHTING B.V., HAARLEM.

contents

Geysir in Haukadalur, the best-known spouting hot spring in Iceland, has given its name to other geysers all over the world. In eruption it ejects a jet of boiling water and steam 50 m up in the air, but now its eruptions occur only very irregularly. Some Icelandic geysers, however, spout quite regularly. The frontispiece features a picture of Hvannadalshnjúkur, the highest peak in Iceland, bathed in the morning sun.

1

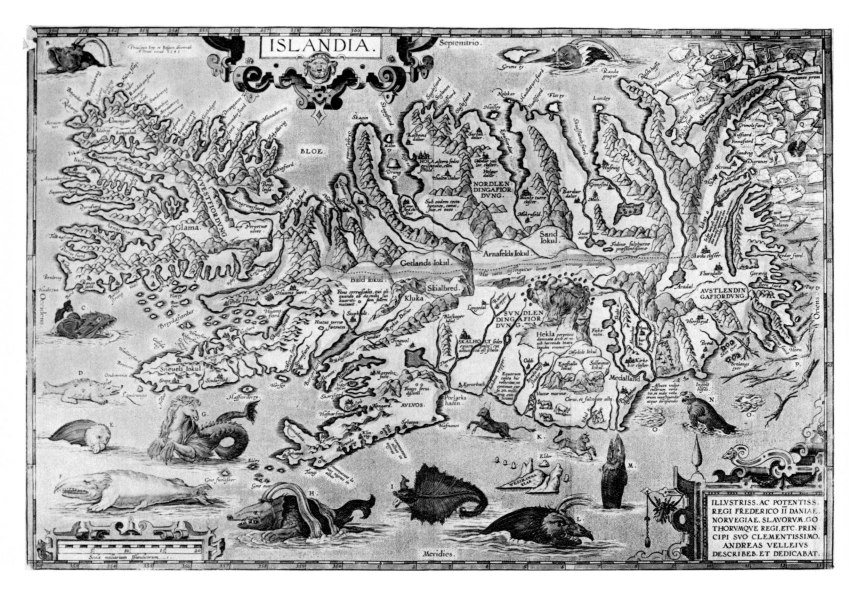

A map of Iceland, made by Bishop Guðbrandur Þorláksson of Hólar before 1585 A.D. The original drawing is lost. The illustration shown is reproduced from a printed version of 1590 which appeared in Additamentum IV, Theatri Orbis Terrarum by Ortelius. The sea ice northeast of Iceland is correctly located with reference to the ocean current boundaries. This is the first map that shows glaciers, and Mt. Hekla is shown to be erupting. The sea monsters, which are included for decorative purposes, were no doubt added by the editor. Bishop Guðbrandur, a pragmatic scholar as he was, is not likely to have appreciated this addition.

land of ice and fire

Iceland is often called a land of ice and fire. It was called Iceland because of the arctic drift ice which since the Norse settlement and down to recent years has occasionally more or less blocked the north-west, north and east coasts. The country could also be named after the glaciers, covering 11.5% of its area. But this northerly island, 103.000 km² (about 40.000 square miles) in area, just south of the Arctic Circle, has got fire below its surface, even below some of its glaciers. These remarkable contrasts of ice and fire are indicated on a map of Iceland, drawn by Bishop Guð-brandur Þorláksson before 1585. On this map the arctic drift ice is shown at Langanes, some glaciers are depicted on a map for the first time, and Mt. Hekla is shown to be erupting. In view of the small population of the country (200.000) and the immense areas covered by lava, volcanic ash, mountains and glaciers, the central highlands of Iceland are essentially virgin nature like an enormous national park. The glaciers and the visits of the arctic drift ice to the shores of Iceland make the name of the country fairly appropriate. At any rate, the Icelandic people appreciate its cold name although it is often emphasised that abroad the name gives a misleading impression of the climate, which is moderately temperate and considerably warmer than the position and the name of the country suggest because a branch of the Gulf Stream almost encircles it.

The settlement of Iceland is considered to have begun around 870 A.D. when the first Norwegian vikings sailed westward with their families and livestock. They found no inhabitants there, except a few Irish monks who had kept the old Greek name, Thule. The Norwegian settlers were accompanied by a number of Scots and Irish. The Icelandic nation, therefore, is basically of Scandinavian origin with an admixture of Celtic stock. In 930 A.D. the vikings established a legislative assembly, the Alþing, at Þingvellir. In 1262 Iceland acknowledged the sovereignty of the Norwegian Crown and together with Norway came under the power of the Danish Crown in 1380. In 1918 Iceland became an independent sovereign state in personal union with Denmark through a common king, but has been an independent republic since 1944.

Ever since the settlement the history of the Icelandic people has been a record of a ceaseless struggle against the elements, severe weather, ice and fire. When drift ice closed the access to fishing and sea transport and spring came late, the cold weather caused great problems. On the other hand, there are 150 volcanoes in Iceland which have been active since the ice age, and about 30 of them have erupted since the settlement. During the last few centuries there have been volcanic eruptions in Iceland every fifth year on the average, and since about 1500 nearly one third of all lava flows on earth have been Icelandic. The country is, therefore, one of the most active volcanic areas in the world, and in the past tephra falls and lava streams caused great damage, such as destruction of vegetation, followed by the death of livestock. When a volcanic eruption occurs under a glacier, the ice above the crater melts rapidly, resulting in floods which sometimes lead to a loss of life, although fatal casualties are less frequent than might be expected. In the volcanic areas of Iceland there are 15 solfatara areas, but hot springs are found at about 700 places. The natural hot water is used for domestic heating on farms, in villages and towns, and for greenhouses.

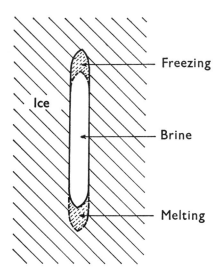

Brine cells can be spotted in ice floes. They are short vertical air-filled tubes in the ice, with both ends closed. They are formed when sea water is trapped in a number of small cavities when sea ice is formed. As more of the water freezes out of this brine, it becomes more and more concentrated and at the same time its specific gravity increases. Therefore, it moves downwards due to gravity and towards a higher temperature. Therefore, these cavities develop into short tubular channels in the ice because freezing occurs at the top of the cell, while melting takes place at the bottom. This phenomenon is indicated on the sketch and shown in the photograph below of a stranded ice floe.

sea ice

Genuine sea ice is formed when the surface layer of the sea freezes. Icebergs, which sometimes drift towards Iceland with the sea ice, come mainly from the Greenland glaciers. The icebergs, therefore, are developed on land by snow falling on the glacier year after year. This snow is in turn transformed into ice under the ever-increasing pressure from above. The valley-glaciers transport this ice into the ocean, and when the sea lifts the glacier snout, it breaks off and a new iceberg floats away. Since 1950 it has been known that a third main type of ice exists in the seas, the so-called ice-islands. In the northern fjords of Greenland and off the north coast of Ellesmere Island thick floating ice sheets are attached to the coasts. These ice sheets are related to both sea ice and land ice. On the top of a sheet of sea ice which has not melted during the summer, snow accumulates year after year and then is gradually transformed into ice under pressure as on inland glaciers. These ice sheets, mainly consisting of fresh water ice, can reach a considerable thickness. When part of this ice sheet breaks off, an ice-island is born. These ice-islands may often be 50 metres thick, 5 metres of which are above sea level. The biggest ice-island discovered so far is about 1000 km^2 in area. These ice-islands are often rather flat on top, but sometimes they have an undulating surface, reminiscent of landscape features. The name is therefore most appropriate, and at first these ice-islands were actually mistaken for real islands.

The ice formed at sea varies owing to different external factors, such as the salinity of the sea, the air temperature, wind and the speed of the formation of the ice. All sea ice consists of pure ice crystals, enclosing a large number of brine cells. If the ice is formed quickly, more brine will be enclosed in the ice. As more and more of the water in the brine cells freezes, the remaining brine will increase in concentration, resulting in increased specific gravity. The brine will, therefore, move downwards in the ice, both due to its weight and its attraction to higher temperatures. These brine cells can be seen in the sea ice floes if carefully looked for. The salinity in the upper part of sea ice is reduced more quickly at increased temperature and the reduction will be very rapid when the temperature comes close to the melting point of the ice. In hummocked ice on top of one-year-old sea ice the salinity is reduced to such an extent that this ice can be melted for drinking water. This fact is of importance for expeditions in polar regions, but experience taught the Eskimos this useful knowledge long ago. The mean salinity of the sea ice east of Greenland is considered to be about $5^o/_{oo}$. It is obvious that the fundamental condition for the formation of sea ice is that the air temperature is lower than the freezing point of the sea, which has been reduced by the salinity of sea water. When the salinity is $35^o/_{oo}$, the freezing point is about $-1.90°$ C. Sea ice is formed much more quickly when the sea is stratified, so that on top of a layer with more salt content, which therefore is heavier, there is a less saline layer. If the difference in specific gravity is sufficient, only very limited mixing can take place between these layers in spite of the sea surface cooling below its freezing point. In this way ice can be formed on the sea although there is much warmer water a few metres below the surface. It is evident, therefore, that layers in the sea are at least as important for the formation of sea ice as low temperature. In the North Polar regions the frost is severe, although not as intense as one might think. The frost very rarely exceeds $-47°$ C., but in the Antarctic $-75°$ C. frost has been recorded. The North Polar region and the surrounding ocean is permanently covered by an almost unbroken sheet of sea ice, several years of age. Following the life of a single ice floe, we find that it starts in the autumn when a

thin layer of sea ice is formed on the surface. During the following winter the thickness increases until it has reached about 2 to 3 metres next spring. During the summer the brine will drain down through the ice floe, forming long vertical brine cells as explained above, and next autumn it has lost a considerable amount of its salt content. The sun melts the surface unevenly and water ponds are formed. The sun warms the water in these ponds more than the dry ice hummocks and therefore more melting takes place around the ponds. Part of the melt-water is discharged into the sea. The following winter additional layers will freeze at the bottom of the ice floe. If the floe survives through the summer, additional layers will freeze to its lower surface the following winter, and this cycle will continue: During the summer ice melts on top of the floe, but the following winter ice will be added at the bottom. After a period of a few years an equilibrium is reached, and while it lasts the thickness of the ice floe will remain 3–4 metres. An ice cube in the floe will thus be moving, from the time it is formed at the bottom, up to the top, where it will finally melt and the resulting water flow back into the sea. Although the mean thickness of arctic sea ice is about 3.5 metres, it can reach a thickness of more than 5 metres.

Scattered ice floes drifting off Straumnes near Aðalvík at the northwest coast of Iceland on March 24th, 1968.

drift ice

A look at a terrestrial globe makes it obvious that there is a great difference between the North and South Polar regions. The South Pole is on a vast continent, mostly covered with ice and snow, about 4800 km wide, surrounded by the Atlantic, Pacific and Indian Oceans. The North Pole, on the other hand, is situated in a large ocean area, about 3200 km wide, but having connections with both the Atlantic and the Pacific Oceans. The North Pole itself is near the middle of this Arctic Ocean, where the depth of the water is about 4000 metres. It was mentioned above

(page 5) that much lower temperature is found in the South Polar region than at the North Pole. The reason is this geographical difference since extreme cold is found above high continents but not above the oceans. In the northern hemisphere the coldest place in winter is not at the North Pole, but in Northern Siberia. The 65° parallel runs through the middle of Iceland, the Norwegian sea, the middle of Norway, through Russia, North Siberia, the Bering Sea, Alaska, Canada, Baffin Bay, Southern part of Greenland and the Greenland Sea. Along this parallel the climate varies enormously. Here we do not only have differences in climate between land and sea areas. The climatic conditions of the sea areas themselves differ substantially. The difference is particularly marked between the eastern and western parts of the Atlantic Ocean. This is clearly indicated on the current map on page 7. The cold Labrador Current is dominant off the east coast of Canada, but the warm Gulf Stream with its extension, the North Atlantic Current and its branches, carries warm water up to the coasts of Iceland and Norway and further on to Spitsbergen and the Barent Sea and therefore keeps the ocean free from ice far to the north. It is mainly due to these warm sea currents that the coasts of Iceland are usually completely ice free most winters and that the climate there is a cold-temperate oceanic climate in spite of the fact that the country is situated just south of the Arctic Circle. But from the North Polar sea comes the very cold East-Greenland Current through the channel between North-Greenland and Spitsbergen which is the main connection between the North Polar region and the North Atlantic Ocean. This current brings large amounts of sea ice which is sometimes carried up to the Icelandic coasts. Therefore, oceanographically Iceland is also a country of contrasts. Off its coasts the cold and warm sea currents meet, the cold Polar Current from the north, and the warm Atlantic Current from the south. Opposite natural forces, air and sea currents, continuously influence the weather with varying

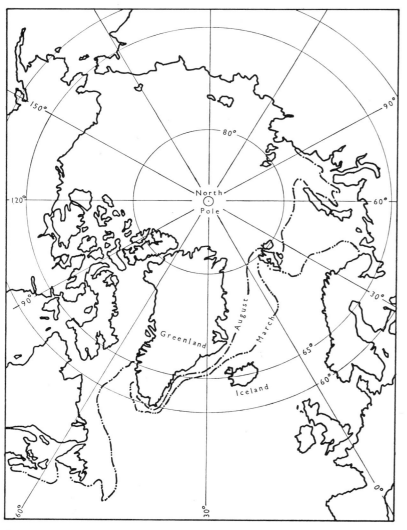

The Arctic is essentially an enclosed sea area, about 3200 km wide, with straits or channels leading to the Atlantic and Pacific Oceans. The map shows the ice border during those months of an average year when the ice has reached its maximum and minimum extent respectively.

effects, resulting in the changeable climate of Iceland. Although an ice cover persists in the Arctic all the year round, it is always on the move and is, therefore, called drift ice. In August the amount of ice is usually at a minimum, but even then it covers an area that is about four times as large as Greenland. In March the drift ice has filled the space up to the coastal ice around the North Polar region, and the sea ice then covers an area twice as large as the ice cover in August. This drift ice is far from being a flat, continuous ice sheet. Due to the action of wind and sea currents the ice is broken up into big or small floes. Since the currents are irregular and the floes vary greatly in size, they move neither at the same speed nor in the same direction. Therefore, open sea is very common between the floes and sometimes there are long narrow leads. In summer fairly large ice-free areas in the drift ice are common where submarines can get to the surface, but when winter comes the floes very soon freeze together. This ice, however, is soon broken into floes again due to the movement of the sea. When no open sea area is left and the drift ice is on the move, the floes either slide over each other or are raised on edge under heavy pressure. Camping on a floe in fast-moving drift ice is, therefore, not without danger. The sea currents are the main moving force, although the wind has also some influence.

Research on the movement of the sea ice in this region started about 85 years ago, first on board ships drifting with the ice, but later by means of floating research stations on ice floes. The first successful expedition by a ship drifting in the ice was the FRAM expedition in the years 1893–6, headed by Fridtjof Nansen. The ship started from the mouth of the river Lena, and for three years it drifted without any damage, locked in the ice, until it got free of the ice near Spitsbergen. FRAM, therefore, drifted over the entire North Polar sea on the Siberian side of the North Pole. In the years 1937–40 the Russian ice-breaker SEDOV drifted along a similar route as the FRAM had done before,

and several other ships have drifted shorter distances, the purpose being to study the movement of the ice. The development of aviation opened up a completely new possibility for this research. The first landing and take-off on an ice floe took place in 1927, but today such landings no longer make headlines as aircraft have brought supplies to several research stations on ice floes or ice-islands, manned by American or Russian scientists for 12 to 18 months at a time. During these periods weather and exact movements of the ice have been registered. Finally, by means of nuclear submarines it is now possible to navigate under the ice across the North Polar region for a closer study of the ocean and of the sea ice from below. Sea ice is a surprisingly plastic material. If the upper surface of an ice floe is covered with ridges and the bottom surface is smooth, then after some time corresponding ridges will develop on the bottom to the extent that every hummock on the top will be lowered until a complete equilibrium is reached when the relief of the bottom is 8 to 9 times as large as the corresponding one on the top.

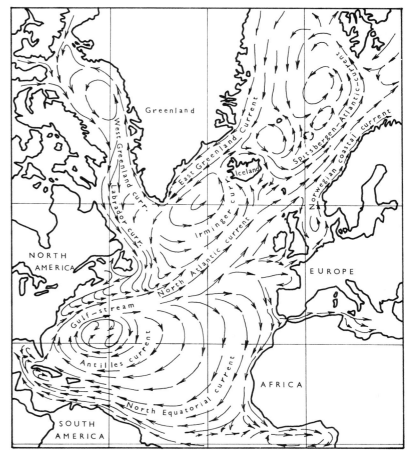

A map of the currents of the North-Atlantic shows how the warm Gulf Stream sends the North-Atlantic Current and its branches up to the coasts of Iceland and Norway, thereby maintaining ice free areas far to the north. The East-Greenland Current, on the other hand, brings with it large quantities of sea ice which sometimes drifts up to the coasts of Iceland.

the sea ice and Iceland

Since the settlement of Iceland the sea ice has been an inevitable part of its history. An account of the settlement of Nordic vikings in Iceland is given in the unique Book of Settlements (Landnámabók). The beginning of the Landnámabók has the following passage: 'In the book of history by the Venerable Bede there is a reference to an island called Thile (Thule), and it is reported in books to be a six days' voyage to the north of Britain; he says there are no days there in winter and no nights in summer when the day is longest. Wise men believe that Thile is Iceland, as in many places in the country the sun shines during the night when the day is longest, and in some places the sun cannot be seen when the nights are longest.'... In the Landnámabók we are also told that before Iceland was settled from Norway there were people in the country, whom the Norwegians called Papar. They were Christians and are believed to have been Irish hermits. It is also said that when Iceland was settled from Norway, Adrianus was Pope in Rome. Adrianus II was Pope in 867–72. The first Nordic men to come to Iceland were the vikings Naddoddur and Garðar Svavarsson. Naddoddur was sailing from Norway to the Faroes when he and his men drifted westward and found a big land. They climbed a mountain on the east coast to look if they could see any smoke or other signs of habitation, but they found none. When they left the country some snow fell on the mountains, and therefore they called the country Snæland (Snowland). – Garðar Svavarsson was of Swedish origin. He went to the Hebrides to fetch his wife's paternal inheritance. When sailing through the Pentland Fjord, wind and sea carried his ship westwards. He came to Iceland, sailed around it, and thus found it was an island. During the winter he stayed at a place he called Húsavík (House-wick). Garðar Svavarsson sailed eastward to Norway. He praised the country and called it Garðarshólmi. – A viking called Flóki Vilgerðarson sailed from Ryvarden in Norway to search for the Garðarshólmi. First he sailed to the Shetland Islands and then to the Faroes. From there he sailed to Iceland, passed Snæfellsnes, then crossed Breiðafjörður and landed at Vatnsfjörður on Barðaströnd. On his Iceland voyage we have the following passage in the Landnámabók (Manuscript: Sturlubók, AM 107 fol.): 'Then fish was abundant in the fjord, and they were so busy catching it that they forgot to make hay during the summer and therefore all their livestock died the following winter. The spring was rather cold. Then Flóki Vilgerðarson climbed a high mountain, and from there he could see a fjord filled with drift ice, and therefore they called the country Iceland, which has been its name ever since.' Close to a river in the Vatnsfjörður there still remain foundations of old walls, believed to be from the buildings erected by Flóki Vilgerðarson when he spent a winter there about the year 856 A.D. Usually there is not much snow at this place, Barðaströnd, and drift ice is very seldom found there. Flóki Vilgerðarson could have seen drift ice from the mountains near Vatnsfjörður and also in Patreksfjörður or Arnarfjörður (see picture on p. 86). It is, however, more likely that he explored the land further and saw drift ice on Steingrímsfjörður or Húnaflói. Nothing is more reasonable than calling the country Iceland after having seen a fjord like Steingrímsfjörður filled with drift ice (see picture on page 11). The following winter Flóki Vilgerðarson stayed in Borgarfjörður and then returned to

Landnámabók ('Book of Settlements') has been preserved in 5 versions, three of which are old, while two are 17th century copies. A vellum manuscript of Sturlubók, written in the 13th century by Sturla Þórðarson, was destroyed by fire in Copenhagen in 1728, but before the original was sent abroad it was copied by the Rev. Jón Erlendsson of Villingaholt. The illustration is of the page in his copy (AM 107 fol.) which describes the voyage of Flóki Vilgerðarson and his stay in Iceland when he gave it the name which it has borne ever since.

at þeir sa Snæfellz nes þa rædde þar̅ vm. þetta
mun vera mikit land er var havfum þundit. her eru
vatnfaull stor. siþ er þat kallaðvr faxa os. þar
flóki siglðu vestvr yfer Breiðafiorð. ok toku þar
land sem heiter vaz fiorðvr við Barða strávnd. þa
var fiorðvrin̅ fullvr af veiðiskap. ok gaðu er eigi þvr'
veiðvm at þa heyiarna ok do allt krikfie þeim vm vetr̅in
voz var helldvr kallt. þa gekk flóki vppa fiall eitt hátt
z sa norðvr yf̅ fiollin fiorð fullan af hafisum. þ̅ kaull
uðu þeir landit Jsland sem þ heper siþ heitit.
þr̅ flóki ætluðu brutt vm sumarit. z vrðu buner litlu
þ vetur. þeim beit ei fyr̅er Reykianes z sleit fra þeim
batin̅ z þar a Heriolf. h̅n tok þar sem nv heiter Heriolfs
havfn. Flóki var vm vetur i Borgarfirði. ok
fundu þr̅ Heriolf. þeir siglðu vm simarit ept'z Nor
egs. Ok er m̅ spurðu af landinu þa let flóki illa yfer
en Heriolfvr sagðe kost z laust af landinv. En þor
olfvr buað driupa smior af hveriu strae a landinu
þvi er þr̅ haufðu þundit. þvi var hn̅ kallaðvr þor
olfvr smior.

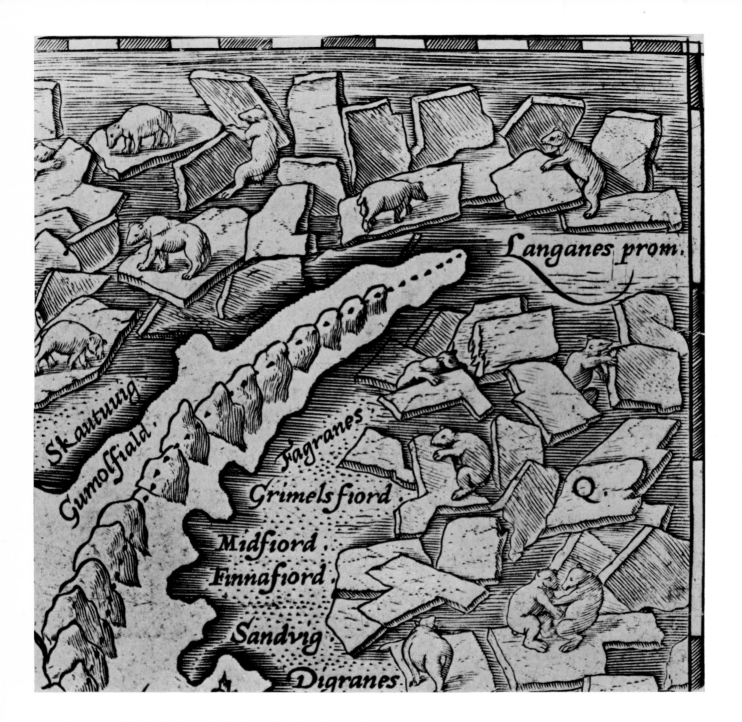

Part of a map of Iceland, drawn by Bishop Guðbrandur Þorláksson before 1585. It shows sea ice and polar bears off Langanes. In explanations under Q on the back of the map it is stated that great quantities of sea ice are carried by currents from the ice-covered ocean to the coasts of Iceland. The movement of the ice floes is said to cause a great deal of noise, and that some of them are crowded with polar bears at play. The entire map is featured on page 2. The place names are easily recognizable, although the lithographer seems to have corrupted the original manuscript in respect of some.

Landnámabók (Book of Settlements) states that Flóki Vilgerðarson gave Iceland its name after climbing a high mountain from which he saw across the mountains in the north a fjord full of ice. It is only natural that he gave the country this name if he saw a fjord like Steingrímsfjörður as it appears in this picture, taken on May 8th 1969.

Norway. He spoke ill of the country, but his men reported both its good and bad features.

The first settlers in Iceland must have got acquainted with the drift ice right from the very beginning, and Icelandic poets have called it 'the old foe of the land'. Most likely the first settlers soon discovered that the name of the country had an adverse influence on immigration, and therefore they named the next country Greenland when they later, about 985–86, continued further westwards because they believed more people would like to leave Iceland for the new land if it had an attractive name.

It is believed, however, that the sea ice did not do much harm during the first few centuries after the settlement, which started about 870. News was brought to Norway about the good land to the west. It was said that Iceland was covered with woods from the sea to the mountains. Fish was plentiful in the fjords and salmon and trout abounded in rivers and lakes. There was also an abundance of birds and eggs and driftwood all over the shores.

It is usually said that the settlement period was over by the time the Alþing, the legislative assembly, was established at Þingvellir about 930 A.D. In the year 1000 Christianity was adopted by law at the Alþing, and when the collection of tithes was begun by the church in 1096, the total population of the country is estimated to have been 70–80 thousand people. When the Icelanders accepted allegiance to the King of Norway in 1262, the old Icelandic commonwealth and the so-called golden period of Iceland's history came to an end. It is generally assumed that during this period considerable prosperity prevailed in the country, and this was the time that generated all the celebrated Icelandic family sagas. It was followed by times of great difficulties and hardship. Volcanic eruptions caused a loss of life and property and the sea ice visited the shores more frequently. Old annals frequently describe these tribulations. People who rely for their living to a considerable extent on livestock are generally very dependent on the weather and other environmental factors. In 1380 Iceland, together with Norway, came under the Danish Crown. All foreign and domestic trade was monopolized by the Danes between 1602 and 1787. Therefore, external circumstances and weather conditions combined to make very hard times for the Icelandic nation. But the 19th and 20th centuries brought great improvements with increased self-government and eventual independence together with more versatile industries and progressively improved technical skills as well as a milder climate. It is important to bear in mind these historical facts when we look to the past in an attempt to study the visits of the drift ice to the coasts of Iceland. It is evident that from the very beginning the Icelanders became familiar with much of the nature of the drift ice north of Iceland and on the seafarers' routes from Iceland to the new settlements on the west coast of Greenland. In the book Konungsskuggsjá ('The King's Mirror'), dating from about 1260, there is a very interesting passage on the drift ice off Iceland: '…when going far enough out into the high sea, we come upon such large amounts of ice in the sea that I do not know any other similar place in the whole world. Parts of this ice are so flat they must have frozen on the sea itself, eight to ten feet thick, and they extend so far from the coast that a journey on foot from land to the edge of the ice would take four days or more… This ice is of a peculiar character. Sometimes it does not move at all, the floes being separated by open sea or fjords, but sometimes their speed is so high that they move no slower than a ship sailing before a good wind. And when they move, they sail just as often against the wind as before it. Some of the ice in the ocean is of a different shape. The Greenlanders call it 'tumbling glaciers'. Their form is like that of big mountains, rising up above the sea level, but they keep company with any other ice although sometimes they travel by themselves'.

This description of the ice floes and icebergs is in many ways correct. Then, as now, the drift ice followed the east

◁

Sea ice is also endowed with certain beauty, both in form and colours, although the cold it brings usually comes first to one's mind.

coast of Greenland, and the movement of the ice was a riddle that long beggared solution.

Historical information on the sea ice off Iceland varies a good deal. Sources from written stories about persons and places are naturally of limited value as they only describe climate and drift ice in relation to certain happenings. Although such information may certainly be very interesting as evidence of the movement of the sea ice up to the Icelandic coast, its value is not extensive in view of the amount of sea ice approaching the coast from year to year. The annals, therefore, are in this respect better sources, and not many other places in the world are likely to have more reliable information on sea ice over such a long period of time. Of course, the interest of the different annalists in the climate and in sea ice varies substantially at different times and places. Therefore, a great deal of work is required to evaluate the sources in such a way that the most correct general view is obtained. The annals use language sparingly, but they contain concentrated information. Lögmannsannal can be quoted as an example: Year 1371: Rather serious famine and a hard winter. Year 1374: Winter and spring so hard that no one could remember anything like it in Northern Iceland. No growth of grass, sea ice at the coast until Bartholomew Mass on August 24th. Year 1375: Winter so good that no one could remember another like it.

There is a marked gap in the information on the drift ice off Iceland during the 15th century and the beginning of the 16th. One of the best extant general accounts of sea ice, however, is to be found in the description of Iceland by Oddur Einarsson, which he wrote in Latin about 1590. This book he called: 'Qualiscunque descriptio Islandiae'. There he writes the following about the drift ice at the end of the 16th century: '…large amounts of it sometimes drift up to the coasts of Iceland so that those who live on the north coast of the country are never safe from this most unwelcome guest. The sea ice drifts all the time between Iceland and Greenland even though it is sometimes by the special grace of God hindered from reaching the Icelandic coasts for several years. When it is close to the coast for a long time, its proximity causes much misfortune for people inhabiting neighbouring areas due to scarcity of grass growth as all fertility disappears from the soil. The nourishing soil juice dwindles as soon as the ice has reached the shores and the cold and raw weather spreads over the land. This island would no longer be inhabitable if it met with such calamity every year. But thanks to Divine Providence the sea ice is kept away so that it does not come near Iceland except when God has decided to punish our nation at irregular intervals, as sometimes there is hardly any trace of sea ice for a decade or more. Sometimes it arrives every fifth year, sometimes every other year, but sometimes it comes two or three times in one year and then with such power and speed that it does not fall behind a ship sailing before a favourable wind. Although one day it cannot be seen from the highest mountains, the following day it may have filled all bays and fjords and spread all over, so that those who look over the ice might think that all the ice from the oceans had been gathered together off the Icelandic coast as it completely covers all the sea north of Iceland so that its limits are nowhere to be seen. Often it drifts around for a long time, more or less of it, like some kinds of floating islands. It matters a great deal at which time of the year it arrives. If it comes in the autumn or in winter when the soil is frozen by virtue of the cold state of the land, the proximity of the sea ice is not so harmful. But if it comes in summer or in springtime, when the features of winter are giving way to sunshine and warmth in the air and the hopes for new growth are developing in the minds of the people, it is certainly an unwelcome guest as it is always followed by a dearth of grass. Therefore, those who live in the southern part of the country are much more fortunate than those in the north as the sea ice is never seen off the south coast. If the sea ice threatens

An aerial view of a patch of ice drifting in the open sea. Some of the floes are of the type called 'pancake ice', i.e. approximately circular floes 30 cm to 3 m in diameter with raised rims, due to the pieces striking against each other.

JAN	FEB	MAR	APR	MAY	JUNE	JULY	AUG	SEPT	OCT	NOV	DEC

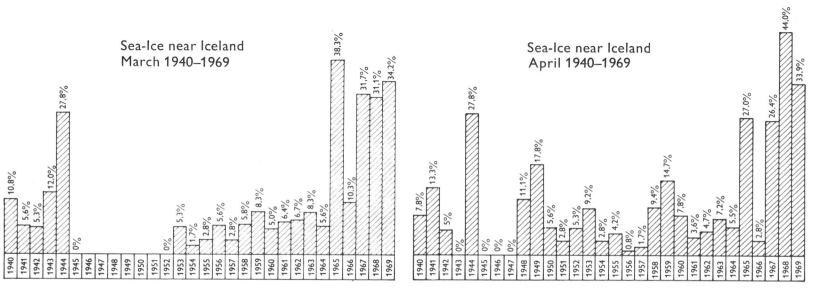

Sea-Ice near Iceland
March 1940–1969

Sea-Ice near Iceland
April 1940–1969

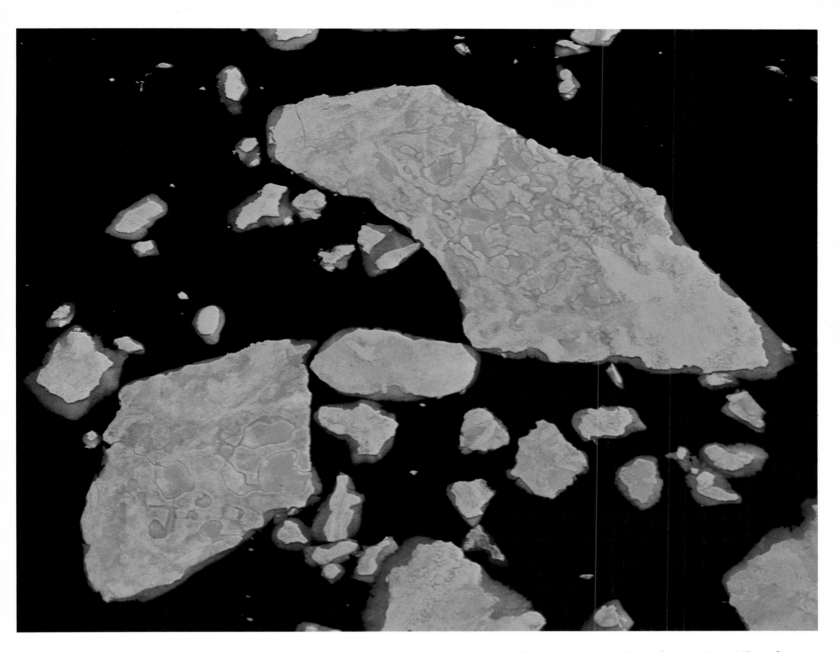

An aerial view of ice floes with ridges of ice and puddles of water. Considerable melting by the sun takes place on the surface. The sun heats the puddles more than the drier ice ridges so that melting is more rapid in and near the puddles.

The picture at the top of page 16 show the distribution of sea ice off Iceland month by month in the years 1960–69. These charts were made by Hlynur Sigtryggsson, Director of the Icelandic Meteorological Office, on the basis of ice reconnaissance during the decade in question, indicating areas where sea ice was seen at some time during each month. At the bottom of page 26 there is a graph comparing the extent of sea ice during the months of March and April in the period 1940 to 1969 indicating the percentage of the total area of the ice charts which at some time during the months were covered by sea ice. These graphs should, therefore, afford a rough comparison of the amount of ice in different years within the area covered by the map.

Sea ice has reached the shores at Hornbjarg, making navigation difficult. This picture was taken during a reconnaissance flight in snow
showers on March 24th 1968. Hornbjarg is a majestic mountain, not
least when viewed from the sea with its precipitous cliff-face right
down to the sea. To the extreme right in the picture is Horn, then
Miðfell and finally Kálfatindur. The rock formation of Hornbjarg
reveals the same beauty in summer and winter, but in summer the
contrast between the steep and grassy slopes of Yztidalur and the
sheer rock-face near by is more pronounced. But this picture was taken
when sea ice and snow showers dominated the scenery.

to close the east or west coast, it is immediately carried away by the powerful currents of the ocean'.

In the 17th century the annals describe the visits of drift ice to the coasts of Iceland in greater detail, and after that the written sources are considered fairly reliable. In his work 'Climate in Iceland during One Thousand Years', published in Copenhagen in 1916–17, Þorvaldur Thoroddsen based his studies on the annals of the past few centuries. Later authors have to a very great extent based their work on this valuable book, which Thoroddsen said he had worked on in his spare time for more than 30 years.

In the late 19th century information on sea ice is collected independently of other events, and here again Þorvaldur Thoroddsen is a pioneer. At the turn of the last century international dissemination of information on sea ice in the North Atlantic started. Then, of course, the gathering of data was limited to observations from the shores and from ships. On the basis of this information ice maps were drawn and subsequently published. As soon as the Icelandic Meteorological Office was established in 1920, it started collecting drift ice information from Icelandic navigated waters. During the last world war ice reports were received from Icelandic fishing vessels, but most other information on sea ice was considered to be confidential, and still some of these sources may not have been found. For almost 20 years after 1944 sea ice was very seldom seen near the Icelandic coasts, although it could sometimes be seen a long distance off the coast. Therefore, many Icelanders lost their interest in the drift ice as it was believed by many that it no longer constituted a threat to their country. The well-known meteorologist and glaciologist, Jón Eyþórsson, did, however, continue to collect valuable information on sea ice, and he published drift ice reports in Jökull, the publication of the Iceland Glaciological Society. The illustration at the top of page 16 shows the distribution of sea ice month by month during the years 1960–69. These maps were compiled by Hlynur Sigtryggsson, Director of the Ice-

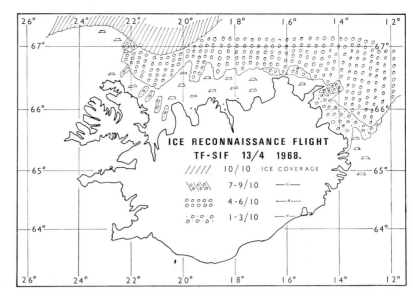

The illustration above is an ice chart based on a reconnaissance flight by TF-SIF on April 13th 1968. The estimated density of the ice is indicated on the chart. Thus, 10/10 coverage denotes that the drift ice covers the sea surface completely, whereas 1–3/10 coverage indicates that one to three tenths of the surface of the sea are covered with drift ice while nine to seven tenths are ice-free. Sometimes single floes are also shown on ice charts. – Below a convoy of ships is sailing through drift ice out of Eskifjörður on the East of Iceland on May 29th 1968. A coastguard vessel is in front, followed by a freighter and four fishing vessels.

landic Meteorological Office. They are based on information that has been collected on sea ice during this decade, and similar maps have been compiled for the years back to 1940. These maps show by shaded areas where ice has been found at any date of each month shown. The density of the ice is not indicated and single floes have been ignored. The basis is a Mercator map with the limits 68° north, 62.5° south, 27° west and 10° east. These maps indicate clearly the extreme limits of the sea ice and its movement month by month during these years. In 1965 there was a lot of ice, and also in 1968 and 1969. Due to regular ice-reconnaissance flights by the Icelandic Coast Guard and more

exact collection of data and comprehensive records on the extent of drift ice north of Iceland during the last one and a half decades, this period is, of course, of much greater value for research and constitutes a more promising basis for ice-forecasts than older sources.

At the bottom of page 16 an attempt is made to compare the amount of sea ice near Iceland in the months of March and April for all the years of 1940 to 1969 by showing statistically the percentage of the area of the ice maps above covered by sea ice sometime during each of these months each year. The months of March and April are usually a period when the sea ice is closest to Iceland, and therefore these statistics should enable us to make a comparison of the amount of sea ice within the map area in the different years.

The sea ice in the vicinity of Iceland has now been considered at some length. It is appropriate, therefore, to look again to the north and east, to the North Atlantic and the Arctic Ocean, where most of the drift ice comes from as mentioned above. It is not likely that man's technology will ever enable him to affect this heavy stream of drift

ice with the East Greenland Current along the east coast of Greenland, but knowledge of the variation of wind and current strength can be useful for an investigation of the possibility of drift ice forecasts for Iceland. Recent research has shown that wind carries ice between the current systems of the Arctic Ocean, and this variation again causes an alteration in the amount of sea ice in the East Greenland Current. As the drifting time for the sea ice from the North Polar Region to the ocean north of Iceland is about one year, it would appear that it might be possible to foresee the amount of sea ice in the East Greenland Current some time ahead, provided it is known that a continuous wind direction has caused transportation of sea ice into the transverse current over the North Pole, which is the beginning of the East Greenland Current. But the amount of sea ice in that current at its origin is far from being a sufficient indication to make possible the forecasting of drift ice to the shores of Iceland. The movement of the drift ice is to a very great extent dominated by the climatic conditions and the sea currents between Iceland and Spitsbergen and still more so between Iceland and Jan Mayen. It is now generally accepted that continuous west and south-westerly winds over the North Greenland Sea can for longer or shorter periods stop or retard the flow of drift ice south along the east coast of Greenland. In this way the amount of sea ice will spread, and the ice coverage north of Iceland will be wider than usual. The meteorological reasons might be the number and directions of passing atmospheric depressions. When the compressed masses of ice start moving again, an altered wind direction and the East Greenland Current could carry the drift ice to the Icelandic shores.

There are still many obscure factors that govern the movement of the sea ice north and east of Iceland, but the visits of sea ice during the last few years have increased the curiosity of scientists. Doubtless further oceanographic and meteorological research will increase our knowledge of drift ice.

◁

Drift ice in bays and fjords cools the sea and upon melting reduces its salinity between the ice floes. Therefore, the open sea between the floes often freezes.

An aerial view of dense drift ice in a low winter sun. ▷

In the past Icelandic poets referred to drift ice as 'the old foe of the land'. Today a number of scientists are eager to increase their knowledge of this unwelcome visitor to be in a better position to prevent its adverse influence on the economy of the Icelandic people.

An aerial view of Drangajökull from the sea on May 29th 1968. Sea ice is still lurking off the coast. All the three nunataks of Drangajökull, Hrolleifsborg farthest to the left, then Reyðarbunga and Hljóða-bunga, can be seen at the head of Reykjafjörður. These are three great rock castles, the biggest of which is Hrolleifsborg, which is 851 m high. Great rock walls extend to the north, but to the south they disappear underneath the glacier.

This is a view from the top of Hljóðabunga to Reyðarbunga and to the Drangajökull glacier. Maps dating from 1911–1914 show Dranga-jökull to be approximately 200 km², but like other Icelandic glaciers it has shrunk appreciably in the last few decades and now it is approxi-mately 165 km² in area. It is, however, still the fifth biggest glacier in Iceland. Reyðarbunga was ice-covered at the turn of the century. Then it emerged like the back of a whale, which is actually the literal meaning of its present name, given by Baldur Sveinsson, then the owner of Þaralátursfjörður.

glaciers

From the beginning of the settlement of Iceland its glaciers with their snow-white caps against the blue sky have been acclaimed for their majestic beauty. That is how they are referred to in many a poem, and the Icelandic nation has certainly got to know their many different aspects during eleven centuries of cohabitation. It even appears that the Icelanders were in fact the first to understand the development and nature of glaciers. If the material written about glaciers in Icelandic had been published in a world language, some of the findings based on the studies of local farmers would have been considered a remarkable contribution to the glaciology of the time.

There is no doubt that some of the Norwegian settlers did know glaciers in their homeland, and in Iceland some of them settled very close to the glaciers. Routes between farms were from the beginning in many places along the edge of glaciers or even across glaciers. No wonder the Icelanders in time acquired some intimate understanding of this phenomenon of nature. At the time of settlement there was most likely a period of mild climate in Iceland, and therefore glaciers were then smaller than they became later on. Thus, the settler Þórður Illugi is known to have built his farm at the foot of Breiðamerkurfjall (lit. 'Breiðamerkur Mountain') between the outlet glaciers Fjalljökull and Breiðamerkurjökull about 900 A.D. (see picture on page 80), but his farm Fjall was buried under a glacier during the years 1695 to 1709.

It is well known that a glacier is a mass of ice, covering mountains or valleys all the year round, the ice being formed naturally from compacted snow. It is evident that a glacier will be formed only if more snow falls during winter than is melted away during the summer. Often snow remains in valleys or depressions although the mountain tops and ridges close by become ice-free in summer. It has been calculated that glaciers cover 11800 km², or about 11.5% of the area of Iceland. By far the biggest of the Icelandic glaciers is the Vatnajökull, which is about 8400 km² in area. The next in size are Langjökull 1020 km², Hofsjökull 996 km², Mýrdalsjökull 700 km², Drangajökull 200 km², Eyjafjallajökull 107 km², and Tungnafellsjökull 50 km². Other glaciers in Iceland are less than 30 km² in area.

The oldest written source on Icelandic glaciers is Saxo's famous Danish History, written about 1200 A.D. It also contains a general description of Iceland which he doubtless based on Icelandic information. After having described the sea ice, Saxo writes: 'There is also another type of ice, covering areas between mountain ridges and peaks, and it is considered that this type of ice changes its position according to a certain rule, with a kind of circulating movement, so that the uppermost layer sinks down to the bottom and the lowest parts move up to the top'. This is by far the oldest explanation of the movement of outlet glaciers, and to a certain extent it is correct as far as ice movements at their foot is concerned. Saxo also tells of people who had fallen into a crevasse and were later found dead on the surface of the glacier. This story is most likely based on actual facts as it was quite common for people living south of Vatnajökull to pass over the tongue of an outlet glacier to get from one farmstead to another. The postman Jón Pálsson was lost on 7th September 1927 when he, together with four horses, disappeared into a deep crevasse on his way over the Breiðamerkurjökull when a narrow snow bridge broke at a spot where the glacial river Jökulsá emerges from under the glacier. On the 15th April the following year his body was found together with his horses on the surface of the glacier near the place where the accident occurred. 'The glacier delivers back what it takes', is an old Icelandic saying. The main reason is the rotational

On a bright summer day the view along Kaldalón valley to Drangajökull is beautiful. The dark-brown glacial river Mórilla emerges from under the outlet glacier and meanders down the valley between old moraines. It is said that in 1840 the outlet glacier covered all this area and that the farm Lónhóll was destroyed by a glacier burst in 1741. In the bottom part of Kaldalón there are gravel plains and moraines with very little vegetation, but further out and on the slopes there is beautiful vegetation, grassland, heather and birch shrubbery.

Fláajökull in Suðursveit is one of the outlet glaciers from the eastern part of Vatnajökull. (see map on p. 48). This is how the snouts of outlet glaciers with their gaping crevasses often look as the ice melts, but the melting is all the time compensated by more ice advancing form under the pressure of the ice cap above.

This is the beginning of an ascent of Drangajökull from Kaldalón on a beautiful summer day. The view is away from the glacier over Kaldalón to Ísafjarðardjúp. If the ascent is made from Votubjörg to the south of Kaldalón the crevasses can be by-passed to a large extent. Good care must be taken, however, as always on glaciers because crevasses may be covered with freshly fallen snow. More dangerous still are the glacier pot-holes, which are funnel-shaped water channels in the glacier ice.

movement of the ice masses in an outlet glacier, which had been known to the Icelanders for centuries before foreign glaciologists noticed it.

The first map in the world to show glaciers by means of special markings is the map of Iceland by Bishop Guðbrandur Þorláksson of Hólar. This map was drawn before 1585 and published in the map collection by Ortelius in 1590 (see figures on page 2 and 129). In this connection it should be mentioned that travelling across the Icelandic highlands was common in former days, and it is considered certain that fishermen even frequently crossed the Vatnajökull glacier in the 15th and 16th centuries on their way between their homes in the north and the fishing centres south of the glacier. It is well known that the subglacial volcano Grímsvötn ('Grim Lakes') on Vatnajökull (see map on page 48 and description on page 54) got its name before 1600, and only an eye-witness could have given it this name. In his glaciological treatise of 1695 the headmaster of the Skálholt School, Þórður Þorkelsson Vídalín, describes the nature of glaciers. He quite clearly got a good deal of his knowledge from people living in close proximity to glaciers. He does not always accept their views, however, although in many cases they have proved to be more correct than his own. He says people believe that in winter more snow is accumulated in the mountains than is melted in summer because the mountains are colder than the lowlands. Therefore the glaciers are subjected to heavy pressures and spread down on to the lowlands. Vídalín also tells of a two days' journey, made by a farmer named Jón Ketilsson from his farm south of Vatnajökull to its northern edge and back again. This trip was made about the middle of the 17th century and is, therefore, most likely one of the very first known explorations of a glacier. One of the most important works on glaciology in the 19th century is the Glacier Treatise by Sveinn Pálsson (1762–1840). Sveinn Pálsson studied medicine and natural history at the University of Copenhagen, and he wrote in Danish his Treatise on Glaciers during the years 1792–94 when he was back in Iceland, making several scientific expeditions at the same time. His work remained unpublished and completely forgotten until part of it was published in 1882, but it was not published in full until 1945, when it was translated into Icelandic by Jón Eyþórsson, forming part of The Travels of Sveinn Pálsson. In his work Sveinn Pálsson puts forward the theory that glaciers move like a plastic mass. This he based on his own observations of the Breiðamerkurjökull Glacier in 1793, and he was convinced that this theory was correct when he was the first to climb the Öræfajökull on 11th August, 1794. In his diary Sveinn Pálsson writes on his ascent of this glacier: 'My attention was mainly drawn to the outlet glacier mentioned above, which moves downwards just east of the farm Kvísker. The surface of this glacier was covered with circular stripes across it, especially near the glacier, and these ogives were bent towards the lowland, indicating that this outlet glacier was actually flowing in a half-melted state like a thick plastic mass. Would this not indicate, in fact, that the ice by its very nature is semi-liquid and flows – without melting – like some types of harpix as I mentioned in the last chapter?'.

Quite clearly Sveinn Pálsson did not know that the Frenchman A.C. Bordiers had then already 20 years earlier published a paper, in which he advanced similar ideas, viz. that glaciers move like a plastic mass. This glaciological work by Sveinn Pálsson stands out as an achievement of a high order as well as the central point of a glaciology which may be looked upon as specifically Icelandic since it was based on the experience of Icelanders of Icelandic glaciers. Simultaneously and independently glaciology was developed in the Alpine region, which later became the basis of the international glaciology of today. For a time Icelandic glaciology even led the way, but it was later completely forgotten until a few decades ago when Iceland again became a centre of interest for glaciologists.

On Drangajökull glacier on Whit-Sunday, June 5th 1938. Hrolleifsborg is straight ahead, but to the right is Reyðarbunga, covered with snow. The picture below was taken on the same spot on August 21st 1966. Hrolleifsborg is to the left and Reyðarbunga to the right. The glacier has quite clearly shrunk during the intervening 28 years, even though it must be taken into account that the older picture was taken earlier in the year.

An overnight camp on Hrolleifsborg on Drangajökull at a height of 851 m. Reyðarbunga and the ice-cap of Drangajökull (925 m) are in the background.

outlet glaciers

It is known that a glacier is formed in places where the annual snowfall exceeds the amount of snow and ice that is lost by melting during the warm season. The snow that falls on an ice cap changes gradually. Most of the snow falls during winter when one layer after another is formed. The accumulation of snow, however, varies with temperature and weather conditions. When the snow melts and freezes again, especially during spring and autumn, ice layers commonly appear between the snow layers. When it rains or the snow is melting, melt-water flows into the lower layers and alters their structure. The snow crystals increase in size, assuming ice-like properties, partly due to the pressure from the snow above. In this way the snow gradually turns into firn. This is explained in greater detail on page 62. A snow pit dug on an ice cap like Bárðarbunga or Öræfajökull (see map on page 48) will readily show up the ice layers and illustrate how glacier ice is transformed into firn. Finally, there are coarse layers of snow, often in conjunction with more dense ice layers. These are layers from the previous summer and autumn, and if the pit is dug near the edge of the glacier, layers of sand or dust, carried up to the glacier by the wind during summer or autumn, may also be found.

But why do not glaciers grow higher each year since a 4 to 8 metre thick snow layer may be added on to the ice cap in one year? Here we come to the crux of glaciology. As Sveinn Pálsson discovered and explained quite correctly in his glaciological work of the 18th century, the reason is that although ice is hard and fragile, it has considerable plasticity like harpix or pitch. Glaciers have their discharge like most lakes. Glacier ice is softer than a layer of sea ice,

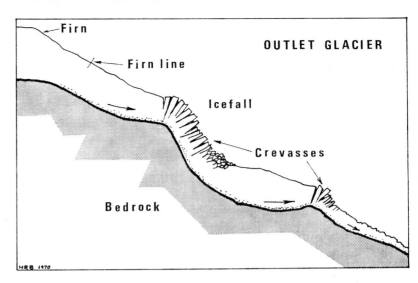

Outlet glaciers drain the ice caps, the pressure of which pushes the ice down to lower levels where it melts until an equilibrium at the snout is reached between melting and the advance of the ice. Crevasses develop where the ice passes over uneven bedrock, making passage difficult and necessitating crampons, ice-axes and ropes.

◁
These are the glacial waters of the river Morilla as seen from Votubjörg to the south of Kaldalón. Their dark-brown colour contrasts sharply with the clear-blue puddles in hollows between old moraines of the outlet glacier. Green vegetation and the barren desert, contrasts of Icelandic nature, meet here, providing a magnificent camping-site.

These are crevasses in the outlet glacier of Langjökull where it extends its snout into Lake Hvítárvatn. Langjökull is the second biggest glacier in Iceland, its size being 1020 km² as measured on maps of 1939. At the present time it is somewhat smaller.

In the last few decades Langjökull has created the so-called jökulborgir ('glacier castles') above Lake Hagavatn. These huge ice edifices are apparently formed when a moving ice cover passes over uneven bedrock.

and therefore glacier ice moves slowly under the pressure of its own ice caps from the mountains down valleys below the firn-line, where the temperature is higher and melting is more rapid than in the highlands. Air temperature falls by about 0.5–0.7° C. on the average for every 100 metres we go up in altitude above sea level. Hence, there is often snowfall in the mountains when it is raining in the lowlands. Each area has an equilibrium at a certain altitude above sea level. Above that altitude snow will accumulate year after year, forming a glacier, but below that same altitude the winter snow will melt away during summer. This yearly melting-limit is called snow line, whereas its mean altitude over a period of some years is called firn line. The firn line lies at very different heights in Iceland. For example, at the southern edge of Vatnajökull the firn line is 1000 to 1100 m above sea level, but at the northern edge of that same glacier the firn line is at an altitude of 1200 to 1400 m as the north side is sheltered from the wettest wind direction. On Drangajökull in the Vestfirðir area (the North West) the firn line usually lies at an altitude of 600–700 m.

It is noteworthy, incidentally, that the term skrið-jökull ('a moving glacier') was originally only to be found in the Icelandic language, indicating that the Icelanders have for a very long time known the nature of outlet glaciers, which move or slide down under the pressure of the ice masses draining the ice caps, which, in turn, slowly sink as the ice masses below glide down towards the lowlands. An ice cap, therefore, does not increase its height if the climate remains constant, even though more snow is accumulated there every year than the warm season can melt away. Further down the outlet glacier more and more of the ice is melted and at its front the movement and the melting is balanced. This equilibrium, however, can be disturbed. If some years of unusually heavy snowfall are followed by cold summers, an outlet glacier may advance further down the valley or on to the lowlands before an equilibrium is reached again. Conversely, the snout of an

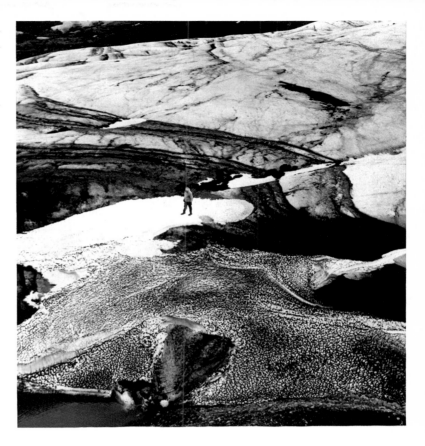

The above picture is of the Sólheimajökull outlet glacier snout where an equilibrium has been reached between advance and melting. Below is the Gígjökull outlet of Eyjafjallajökull glacier where it extends down into a small glacier lake.

◁
In Karlsdráttur at the end of Lake Hvítárvatn there is beautiful vegetation just by the snout of the Langjökull outlet glacier. Mt. Skriðufell is in the background. A few decades ago it was entirely enclosed by outlet glaciers. The maximum depth of Lake Hvítárvatn is 70 m off Mt. Skriðufell.

outlet glacier will retreat if several years of relatively light snowfall are followed by warm summers, and that has been the case of Icelandic outlet glaciers during the last few decades.

By measurements it is possible to study the movement speed of outlet glaciers. It has been found that their speed varies, depending on the cross section, shape and size of the outlet glacier or valley glacier in relation to the height and mass of the ice cap or the inland glacier. Measurements made at the Hoffellssjökull, a south-eastern outlet of Vatnajökull (see map on page 48), have shown that this valley glacier moves up to 630 m a year and that its thickness is about 250 m. A considerable amount of ice is, therefore, transported by the outlet glaciers down to the lowlands if the melting there is fast enough. On the other hand, heavy snowfalls and a big inland ice sheet or ice cap is needed to maintain such a fast movement of an outlet glacier.

The outlet glaciers are, therefore, very readily affected by variations in the ice cap. If several years of cold weather and heavy snowfall occur in succession, the ice cap will grow higher and its outlet increase. Therefore, the outlet glacier will grow thicker and move further on towards the lowland. The lower end of the outlet glacier will then be higher and steeper. A slow-moving or stationary outlet glacier, on the other hand, has a flat snout which consequently is much easier to cross. An end moraine is formed at the front of an outlet glacier either by its grinding action, pushing sand and debris in front of it, or by a stationary outlet glacier, depositing at its foot material transported from the mountains or nunataks in the glacier above. Outlet glaciers also bring down big rocks and gravel frozen in the bottom layers, wearing out the valley floor by an abrasive action, frequently resulting in scratches and rounding off of the rocks. They are called roches moutonnées, due to their resemblance to the backs of sheep. (French mouton, 'sheep'), and the deep scratches

⇧

The edge of the Langjökull glacier is cut by deep crevasses where it extends to the slopes of Jarlhettudalur, a valley which has only recently emerged to a large extent from under the glacier.

⇦

Big rocks are often transported by outlet glaciers from mountains in the highlands down to the lowlands. Under the pressure of the moving ice these rocks scrape the underlying bedrock, producing glacial striae. In many parts of Iceland they offer evidence of the direction in which ice-age glaciers moved. This picture was taken in East-Iceland.

⇨

In the past Lake Hvítárvatn was famous for its icebergs, delivered to the lake by two outlet glaciers. Today only a narrow extension of the more northerly outlet glacier reaches as far as the lake so that only a few scattered icebergs are to be seen there now.

⇨

Although the Langjökull outlet glacier at Hvítárvatn is not of the same dimensions as it used to be, it is still quite impressive on closer inspection. Many fantastic ice formations are to be found in the churned-up ice masses.

Many of the crevasses in the Langjökull outlet glacier are gigantic. Slowly the ice makes its way down to Lake Hvítárvatn. No movement can be discerned by people walking on the outlet glacier, but now and then there are big thuds and bangs.

⇨

To the south of Arnarfell hið mikla an outlet glacier extends from Hofsjökull down to Þjórsárver. This outlet glacier dams up a glacier lake which is filled with water in early spring. Ice floes break off the outlet glacier and float on the lake until it is empty in early summer. The remaining floes then often make up the most grotesque ice formations.

⇧

This is a view from Norðurjökull, an outlet glacier of Langjökull, over to Kerlingafjöll. Karlsdráttur is to the left.

38

The picture above is a view over the river Þjórsá and Þjórsárver to Hofsjökull and Arnarfell. Arnarfellsjökull is a beautifully shaped glacier which extends from Hofsjökull down to Þjórsárver, which is a continuous grass-covered area at the south-eastern edge of Hofsjökull. Þjórsárver is to some extent a tundra because the subsoil is often frozen all summer. This area is the world's biggest colony of the pink-footed goose with about 9000 pairs nesting there.

Below is a view of Mýrdalsjökull where one of the most active volcanoes of Iceland, Katla, rests under the ice sheet. Katla eruptions produce enormous glacier floods. Katla is apparently situated on a volcanic fissure which is most likely an extension of the Eldgjá fissure. The last Katla eruption occurred in 1918.

produced are called glacial striae. As they generally run in the line of ice movement, they provide an evidence of their existence a long time after the glaciers have withdrawn from the area.

When outlet glaciers retreat, as they have been doing in Iceland for the last 40–50 years, they cause a great deal of alteration to the surrounding landscape. At Lake Hagavatn and in the Jarlhettudalur valley at the edge of Langjökull glacier the landscape has, for example, undergone a radical change. Big pieces of ice may remain for some time buried in clay and sand where the glacier has withdrawn, and walking may be difficult in knee-deep mud on the top of a layer of dead ice, preventing the water from getting away. But vegetation reaches this new area surprisingly quickly, even if there is still ice underneath. In midsummer the vegetation is often so soggy that a man walking in it penetrates to the ice layer.

Gígjökull in the northern part of Eyjafjallajökull goes down to a small glacier lake, which is sometimes dotted with ice floes from the outlet glacier.

Snæfellsjökull

A view of Snæfellsjökull from the south-east. From the lowlands it certainly makes a majestic sight and invites climbing on a fine day. The picture was taken on May 2nd, the snow reaching much farther down the slopes than later in the summer.

Snæfellsjökull is the name of the 1446 m high fascinating ice cap at the extreme end of the Snæfellsnes Peninsula. Even in Reykjavik, 115 km away, this regularly shaped volcanic cone with its snow cap on top makes a grand spectacle. In mid-summer the sun setting behind the golden cap of Snæfellsjökull throws an almost indescribable array of colours over the Faxaflói Bay. On a map of 1910 the glacier is shown to be about 22 km², but its size has shrunk rapidly during the last half century, being now little more than 11 km². After a warm summer long mountain ridges to the south are often free of ice. There has been no volcanic eruption in Snæfellsjökull in historical time, but volcanic craters can be easily seen. The top crater is the biggest one, but it is completely covered by the glacier, not a single stone being visible in the caldera. The edges of the crater, on the other hand, are prominent landmarks because three single rocks, which are parts of the crater edge, are actually very characteristic features of the mountain. In winter and spring they are usually ice-covered, but during summer and autumn the black rocks become visible. Lava must have flowed in all directions down the slopes of the mountain, and around it there are several old craters which at one time emitted lava streams reaching all the way down to the sea.

It is quite easy to climb Snæfellsjökull at any time of the year. In early spring the snow reaches further down the slopes, and therefore walking on snow will be longer. Four to five hours should be allowed for walking from the lowland to the highest peak from the south-west side. The route has very few crevasses in the spring as can be seen in the picture on this page, but when the peak is covered with

A view to the north from the highest peak of Snæfellsjökull. Breiðafjörður is in the background.

⇦

At the highest peak of Snæfellsjökull on May 1st 1967. Snæfellsjökull is an extinct volcano, 1446 m. in height. At the mountain top there are three peaks, two of them precipitous rocks, black in summer and covered with a glassy ice mantle in winter and in spring. Here is a view of the caldera, covered with glacier ice.

ice as it is in these pictures, good crampons are essential. An ice axe and a nylon rope are also recommended, although the crevasses are usually not much open in the spring. In summer and autumn the crevasses are more open near the peaks and on the sides of the caldera of the top crater. As Snæfellsjökull is a very small glacier, its crevasses are always much smaller than those of larger glaciers. The outlet glaciers are also relatively small and slow-moving. Therefore, the Snæfellsjökull presents an excellent challenge to a beginner wanting to acquire experience of the world of glaciers. A tent and good equipment would enable him to spend a few enjoyable days there. Walking along the edge of the crater and climbing all the rocks would take one day. Another day could be spent on an exploration of the top crater and the outside of the ice cap. It would, however, take a somewhat longer time to find the crater opening which in the famous novel by Jules Verne is said to be an entrance to the centre of the earth (Jules Verne: Voyage au centre de la terre, 1864).

⇧
The highest peak of Snæfellsjökull (1446 m), seen from the middle peak. There are few crevasses in early spring, but their number increases as the summer advances.

In clear weather there is a magnificent view from Snæfellsjökull as this peak towers high above its surroundings at the outer end of the peninsula between Faxaflói and Breiðafjörður bays. But even when the sky is not clear enough for these distant views, there are many things of interest on Snæfellsjökull itself and in its immediate vicinity. The enormous variety of rock shape and ice formation near the peak is well worth seeing. The ice varies all the time in shape and structure because its formation is dependent on weather conditions at the time of development. Nature is highly imaginative, indeed, in its form design.

⇦
Glassy ice near the middle peak of Snæfellsjökull on May 1st 1967. There is no way of securing a footing anywhere except by means of crampons. A rope and an ice-axe are also necessary pieces of equipment as always on glaciers.

⇨
The top peak of the Snæfellsjökull glacier, completely covered with glassy ice. In late summer all the ice cover has melted, exposing the black rock.

A Vatnajökull expedition at the foot of Grímsfjall on its way to the Grímsvötn, a volcanic area under the ice of central Vatnajökull.

A train of snowmobiles near the edge of the Tungnaárjökull glacier at the beginning of a Vatnajökull expedition. It is often quite hard to get snowmobiles and luggage to the edge of the glacier because of glacial rivers and mud. Sledges, towed by snowmobiles, are loaded with equipment, provisions and petrol barrels.

On Öræfajökull. A view from Jökulbak (1922 m) to Hvannadals-hnjúkur. the highest peak in Iceland, 2119 m. The snowmobile route from the wide expanses of Vatnajökull to Öræfajökull is through the pass of Hermannaskarð, past Þuríðartindur through the pass of Tjaldskarð, on to Snæbreið (2041 m) and from there to the foot of Hvannadalshnjúkur, which towers almost 250 m above the glacial plain (see map on p. 48).

A train of snowmobiles has reached a mast erected for snow measurements on Vatnajökull. A pit is dug in the ice to measure the thickness of the snow layer that has accumulated in the preceding year and to take samples of the glacier ice at various depths. In the background is the nunatak Pálsfjall.

Vatnajökull

Vatnajökull is by far the biggest glacier in Iceland. Maps of the years 1904 to 1938 indicate its area to be about 8400 km², and although it has shrunk somewhat during the last few decades, it is still almost as big as all the glaciers on the European Continent combined. During the French-Icelandic Vatnajökull Expedition in 1951 the thickness of the ice was measured by means of echo-sounding equipment. Then it was found that the ice is much thicker than was commonly believed before. The measurements showed the thickness of the ice to be 600–800 m. in general, and the greatest ice thickness measured was 1000 m. The main part of Vatnajökull, therefore, rests on a mountainous landscape, made up of valleys and mountain ridges no more than 800–1000 m above sea level. As mentioned before, the firn line at the southern edge of Vatnajökull is at an altitude of 1100 m. Therefore, if the ice cap suddenly melted away, no glacier would be formed again in this area, except for small ice caps on the highest peaks, provided the climate remained the same as it has been during the last 40–50 years. The measurements also indicate quite clearly that in many valleys which are now covered by thick ice there might after some time be fertile farmland. But as the situation is now, the surface of the Vatnajökull glacier is mostly at an altitude of 1400–1600 m above sea level, and therefore this glacial area continues to collect winter snow since it extends well above the firn line. Thus, the greater part of Vatnajökull is a fairly even ice cap or ice sheet, although there are some slight bulges and depressions. The highest ice cap, Bárðarbunga, which is about 2000 m high, is on the north-west part of the ice sheet, its slopes at the western extremity of the glacier being almost precipitous.

In many places the Vatnajökull ice sheet is encircled by border mountains, some of them having peaks reaching high above the main ice sheet and therefore greatly adding to the majestic view of the glacier. Among these border mountains are Kerlingar (1339 m) and Hamarinn (1573 m) to the west, Kverkfjöll (1920 m) to the north, and Hrútfjallstindar (1875 m) and Miðfellstindur (1430 m) to the south. The Öræfajökull ice cap is, in a way, a separate glacier as it is on a much higher level, although it is connected to the main ice sheet of Vatnajökull. Rising out of the main ice sheet of Vatnajökull, there are also some nunataks, single mountains and ridges surrounded by ice, such as Pálsfjall (1335 m) and Grímsfjall (1725 m) in the western part of the Vatnajökull ice sheet, Grendill (1570 m) to the east, Esjufjöll (1522 m) and Máfabyggðir (1449 m) in the southern part, near Breiðamerkurjökull. On the Öræfajökull ice cap there are the nunataks Þuríðartindur (1741

The biggest obstacle in the way of Vatnajökull expeditions from inhabited areas to Jökulheimar, the hut of the Iceland Glaciological Society at the foot of Tungnaárjökull, has until recently been the river Tungnaá. A train of vehicles is crossing the Tungnaá on the Hofsvað ford. Now this river has been bridged further down.

m) to the north-east, Knappar (1758–2044 m) to the east and south, and finally the Hvannadalshnjúkur to the north-west, 2119 m, the highest peak in Iceland. A look at a map of Vatnajökull (see page 48) makes it clear how the outlet glaciers flow out from the ice sheet wherever the border mountains do not prevent their movement down to the lowlands until a balance is reached between the accumulation of snow above the firn line and the flow and melting of the outlet glaciers. Crevasses occur in greatest numbers where an outlet glacier has a high speed, but they are also common high up on the ice sheet above the outlets. Often the best way to climb the glacier, therefore, is to follow a border mountain or a mountain ridge reaching into the interior. Along the western edge of Vatnajökull the outlet glaciers are almost continuous and are only divided by single mountains. These glaciers are called after the rivers issuing from them: Köldukvíslar-

jökull, Tungnaárjökull, Skaftárjökull, and Síðujökull. Along the southern edge there are many border mountains, keeping the glacier closed in so that the outlet glaciers here mostly flow down valleys. The biggest outlet glaciers along the southern edge are Skeiðarárjökull and Breiðamerkurjökull, but some smaller, though very steep, outlet glaciers extend from the Öræfajökull. From the Breiðabunga area there are the Hoffellsjökull, Fláajökull, and Heinabergsjökull. The biggest outlet glaciers extending from the northern edge of Vatnajökull are the Brúarjökull and Dyngjujökull and, finally, the Kverkjökull, a small valley glacier coming out of the Kverkin, a part of an old volcanic crater in Kverkfjöll (see picture on page 103). These Vatnajökull outlet glaciers are not alike. They behave very differently, each of them actually requiring a separate study although they have some characteristics in common. Some of them, such as the Skeiðarárjökull, dam

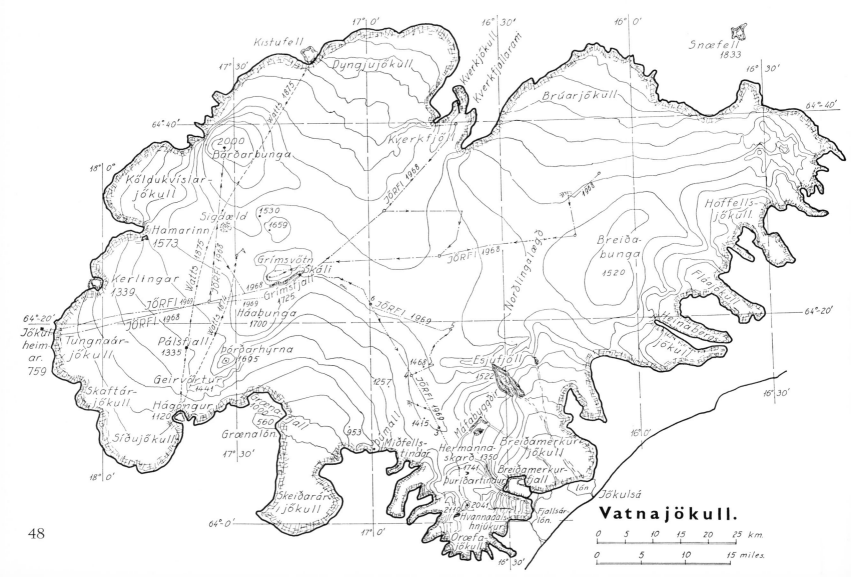

Vatnajökull.

48

up lakes in side-valleys. Such lakes cause jökulhlaup ('glacier floods') when the water is emptied at intervals of some years (see further on page 80–83). The nature of each outlet glacier is, of course, greatly influenced by its surroundings, e.g. the landscape under the glacier, the size and altitude of the ice cap from which it extends, whether mountains limit the width of a valley glacier, and, finally what is of importance for all outlet glaciers, the yearly accumulation of snow above the firn line and the melting below it. The glaciers are slow in their reaction to climatic changes, and therefore such changes have to last for many years before their influence on the glacier becomes evident. However, big and flat outlet glaciers seem to be more sensitive to irregular climatic variations than thick and narrow valley glaciers, confined by mountains on both sides. So far, no theory has been advanced to explain the sudden and often completely unexpected advance of these big and flat outlet glaciers of Vatnajökull. The reason might possibly be a reluctance on the part of the outlet glacier to increase its moving speed evenly due to a frictional resistance of the ground layers, even though increased ice masses on the main glacier require an increased speed of the outlet to maintain an equilibrium. Due to the slow movement of the outlet glacier melting would decrease its thickness higher up than usual. This process might continue until the thin outlet glacier was getting too light to withstand the increasing pressure from the thicker glacier higher up, when it would cause a sudden advance of the outlet glacier which then would move further down than would have been the case if the accumulation of snow each year had been balanced by movement and melting. – This is only a guess, but Vatnajökull is very suitable for a study of the behaviour of this type of outlet glaciers. In point of fact, Brúarjökull advanced suddenly in the winter of 1963–64 up to 8 km. It is also known that Brúarjökull advanced similarly in 1890. In a Vatnajökull expedition in the summer of 1966 a snowmobile partly fell into a crevasse on the

route between Grímsfjöll and Kverkfjöll. The crevasses from the advance of Brúarjökull in 1963–64 were reaching that far, and members of the summer expedition of the Iceland Glaciological Society in 1968 found that there were still crevasses a long way into the glacier as shown on the map on page 48. Regular measurements of variations in the outlet glaciers of Vatnajökull started in 1930. They only cover the southern glaciers, however, and during the last few years also Tungnaárjökull. On the other hand, the outlet glaciers which are shown to have advanced suddenly are all of the big and flat type, mainly in the north and west parts of Vatnajökull. Besides Brúarjökull, the following have had sudden advances: Síðujökull in 1934 and again in 1963–64. The last advance was studied from the air and crevasses and movement were noticed up above Pálsfjall. Skaftárjökull advanced in 1945. Both Dyngjujökull and Síðujökull advanced in 1934, and Síðujökull again in 1951. The total areas of Vatnajökull which have advanced or moved suddenly since 1930, including the advance of 1890, amount to about 40% of the total area of Vatnajökull.

It is believed that fishermen from the north did not cross Vatnajökull after 1575. Someone must have come to the Grímsvötn caldera as mentioned before because this name is very old. However, the crossing of Vatnajökull was apparently not very common in former days and the oldest maps of Iceland indicate that people were entirely unaware of the enormous size of the Vatnajökull area. Therefore, the south-east part of the country always appeared unduly slim on the maps. The northern and southern

To be towed by a snowmobile across the expanses of Vatnajökull is effortless, but exhilarating, for a skier. Nowhere is the sunlight brighter or the air fresher.

↑
A view to the south from snow pit No. 6, indicated on the map on p. 48, on the Vatnajökull ice-cap to the southern border mountains of the glacier, Skaftafellsfjöll. Þumall, a dark-looking basalt rock, is most prominent. It has never been climbed.

⇨
Öræfajökull extends from Vatnajökull in a southerly direction, rising considerably above the main Vatnajökull ice cap as can be seen most clearly when it is viewed from the north (see the map on p. 48). Þuríð-artindur is to the left, then Öræfajökull with the highest peaks Snæ-breið (2041 m) and Hvannadalsknjúkur (2119 m), and then Hrút-fjallstindar, Miðfellstindur and Þumall.

edges of the Vatnajökull glacier were known, but not the very substantial distance between them. – It is not until 1875 that written sources relate of a crossing of Vatnajökull. It was made by a Scottish explorer, W. L. Watts, together with some Icelandic guides. It is clear that Watts principally relied on Páll Pálsson, and he named the nunatak Páls- fjall after his guide, not himself. Watt and his companions tried to cross Vatnajökull in 1874, but had to give it up due to bad weather. In 1875 they went all the way in 12 days. The estimated route of Watt and his company is shown on the map on page 48. Most likely they would not have had to take a route much farther to the east to find the Gríms- vötn caldera, which then were only known by an old tradi- tion.

The next crossing of Vatnajökull was made by two Scots on skis. They spent 22 days on the glacier. A Danish surveyor, J. P. Koch, crossed Vatnajökull with four guides on Icelandic horses in 1912. They came from the north,

found Grímsvötn and made a sketch of the caldera. Two peaks there have since been called Svíahnjúkar ('Peaks of the Swedes'), honouring this first real scientific explora- tion of Vatnajökull. – Due to an eruption in the Gríms- vötn area in 1934 and a consequent glacier flood (jökul- hlaup) in the Skeiðará River, many expeditions went to Grímsvötn in 1934–36 and excellent written sources are available on the research that was done then. A motor- driven sledge was first used on Vatnajökull in 1947 in a trip to Grímsvötn, demonstrating the advantage of motorized means of transport on glaciers. When the aircraft Geysir (a DC 4 passenger aircraft) crashlanded on Bárðarbunga in 1950, an American rescue airplane (a DC 3) was left on the glacier. It was retrieved in the spring of 1951 when bull- dozers were used to dig the aircraft out of the snow and pull it down from the glacier. – The French-Icelandic expedition mentioned above used snowmobiles on Vatna- jökull in 1951. The Icelandic Glaciological Society was

went to Esjufjöll and back again. This was part of a pre- paration for an expedition across the Greenland ice sheet in 1912–13, using Icelandic horses. A member of this ex- pedition was the Icelander, Vigfús Guðmundsson, sub- sequently called Vigfús the Greenland-traveller. In 1919 two Swedes, H. Wadell and E. Ygberg, went on horseback east over Vatnajökull. They passed Pálsfjall and Háabunga

founded in 1950, and since 1953 this society has arranged expeditions to Vatnajökull by snowmobiles every spring and sometimes also in the autumn, measuring snow ac- cumulation at different places. The routes (marked JÖRFI) chosen in 1968 and 1969 are indicated on the map on page 48, some of the research spots also being marked, but the routes have varied somewhat from year to year.

◁
In fine weather Öræfajökull offers beautiful views in every direction. This is a view NNE over Breiðamerkurjökull. Esjufjöll are to the left and Veðurárdalsfjöll to the right. Over Breiðabunga there is a view to the north over the glacier where Snæfell (1833 m) can be spotted faintly, The distance between Öræfajökull and Snæfell is almost exactly 100 km.

the weather

The weather on Vatnajökull can be very changeable, even within the period of a short trip. There may be frost and snow-storms at any time of the year as well as sleet and rain. But there are also days of warm sunshine on Vatnajökull so that there is a great temptation to strip for sunbathing in spite of the danger of sunburn. On a glacier the light is very powerful. When the sun shines, the light is reflected from the white snow so that the sunshine actually comes both from above and below. Then there is the peculiar shadowless light so common on glaciers and only known under similar conditions elsewhere, e.g. in large completely white areas such as in the Arctic or on drift ice. When fog covers the glacier, there is, of course, no real sunshine, but full daylight can still remain even though no shadows can be seen. This is called whiteout, a condition in which daylight is diffused by a multiple reflection between the snow surface and an overcast sky so that everything is snowwhite. There is no difference any more between the sky and the glacier, all contrasts vanish, and it is impossible to spot the horizon or any irregularities or holes in the snow. It is said that in such weather one can easily walk over the edge of a cornice or fall into a crevasse. To observe this completely white world of wonders gives one a feeling that is difficult to describe in words and impossible to register on a photograph in the absence of contrasting shadows.

A camp pitched on the north side of Vatnajökull in fine weather. There is a slight breeze and the night is bright. A sudden snowstorm at a camping site like the one shown below must always be expected, however, so that suitable tents and sleeping-bags are absolutely essential on a glacier.

Sunrise in the westernmost part of Grímsvötn. A view to the north. In the mountain slopes from left to right are Vatnshamar (1495 m), Depill (1455 m), and Stóri Mósi. Down in the caldera there is a black ridge, Naggur, which is completely submerged when the level of the Grímsvötn lake is highest just before a glacier flood. These glacier floods used to occur approximately every 10 years, but now they happen about every 5 years.

◁

The first task to be done on arrival at the hut of the Iceland Glaciological Society on Grímsfjall is to clear the door and the windows of snow. When the wind is blowing and the snow is falling this small and cosy hut, situated on the edge of the Grímsvötn caldera is a most welcome destination.

◁

When it is foggy on a glacier there is sometimes a peculiar shadowless light which is almost unique. Yet, at the onset of a slight breeze, the sun often unexpectedly breaks through the clouds. This picture is taken on Grímsfjall when the fog is making way for sunshine.

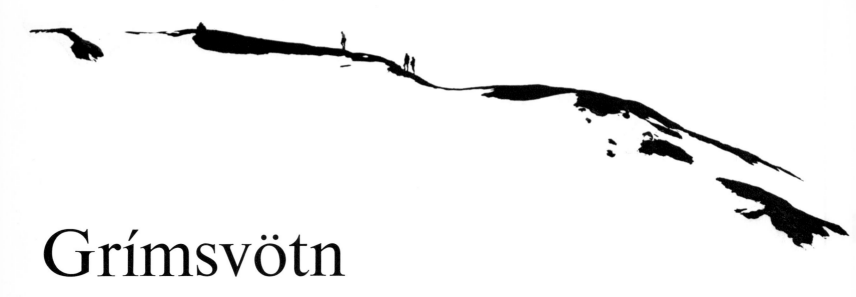

Grímsvötn

Below the ice cover of Vatnajökull there is an active volcanic fire. Most famous of the volcanic areas is the Grímsvötn depression to the west of the central part of the ice cap. This depression is about 35 km² in area and more than 500 m deep. Between eruptions a large amount of water accumulates in it, mainly glacier ice melted by volcanic heat, most likely in the form of solfatara activity. The Grímsvötn lake is an ice-dammed lake, in some respects similar to Grænalón (see pictures on page 82 and 83). The difference is that very little water is seen at Grímsvötn as it is usually covered by a sheet of ice. Before 1934 the Grímsvötn basin was discharged of water nearly every 10th year by a violent glacier burst. The water forced its way below Skeiðarárjökull and flooded Skeiðarársandur for about one week at a time. The maximum amount of water is estimated to have been 50.000 m³/sec. These glacier bursts from Grímsvötn were sometimes accompanied by violent eruptions there. It is not clear, however, if a volcanic eruption is the primary cause of a glacier burst,

or if a volcanic eruption starts after a glacier burst has emptied the basin and reduced the pressure above. Glacier floods (jökulhlaup) are a well-known phenomenon of ice-dammed lakes occurring at fairly regular intervals without any connection to volcanic activity. It is striking how regularly the glacier bursts from the Grímsvötn occurred at intervals of 9 to 10 years, but now they happen at intervals of about 5 years. The level of the Grímsvötn lake rises fairly regularly by 12–14 m a year, or by about 3.5–4 mm a day. This rise of the water level is measured every year during the expeditions of the Icelandic Glaciological Society, the basis of these measurements being a cairn at the nunatak Stóri Mósi in Grímsvötn. In the picture above the surveyors are on their way up to the cairn on the 8th of June 1968. After the big glacier bursts the level of the lake is lowered by up to 200 m. If the theory of an ice-dammed lake is correct, this rise in the water level of the Grímsvötn lake must be needed to build up a sufficient force to lift the ice dam at the mouth of the hanging valley to enable

In the picture above scientists are on their way to the survey cairn on the tuff ridge Stóri Mósi at the inner end of the Grímsvötn depression. The rise of the water level is measured against this cairn. To the right there is a view from Grímsfjall westwards down to Grímsvötn at sunrise. The sun gilds the summit of Grímsfjall and the rocks at the inner end of Grímsvötn, while the ice covered lake is still hidden in the bluish haze of the night.

An excellent long ski-slope extends from the hut of the Iceland Glaciological Society down to Grímsvötn, but sometimes crevasses near the top have to be avoided. The light is reminiscent of the so-called whiteout exemplified by the fusion of the sky and the glacier which eliminates any visible horizon. Although there is no real fog here, it would be hard to estimate any distances if it were not for the skiers seen in the distance. – Below men are standing near Gríðarhorn in the Grímsvötn depression. Hot springs at the foot of the mountain melt the ice and form deep crevasses from which hot vapours stream out, cutting right through the ice layers above.

the water masses to force their way under the ice sheet down the Skeiðarárdalur valley. The last big volcanic eruption in Grímsvötn occurred in 1934, and this is the only eruption which has been studied on the spot shortly after it began and until 1936. The first map based on actual measurements was made by Trausti Einarsson in 1935. – It is now generally believed that volcanic activity is much more common under the Vatnajökull ice cover than was thought in earlier days. This view is based on studies of the glacial rivers issuing from under different areas of Vatnajökull. The subglacial landscape is in many places different from the Grímsvötn area. Volcanic eruptions may take place in a valley or a mountain covered by ice where considerable amounts of lava or tephra may come up to the surface without breaking through the ice cap above. A geographical comparison of Grímsvötn with other volcanic areas near the glacier shows that the Grímsvötn area is on a line connecting the Kverkfjöll and Laki. In recent years an ice cauldron ('sigdæld') has developed north-west of Grímsvötn (see map on page 48). It is considered likely that a subglacial eruption took place there in 1955 and also later in view of the increased amount of water in, and sulphur smell from, the glacial river Skaftá, the water outlet from this area

Below Gríðarhorn there is no need to dig pits to study a profile of the Grímsvötn ice layers because the heat cuts right through the firn. The thickness of the ice cover can be estimated from the height of the man.

research

This 8 m deep ice pit vas dug on Öræfajökull at a height of 2041 m on May 27th–29th 1969. Then a hand-drill was used to extract ice cores further down from its bottom for the purpose of analysis. Continuous samples are taken in metal cylinders from the top to the bottom of the pit wall.

Glacier research has a multiple purpose, one of the main objects being to study the changes glaciers undergo, their advances or retreats, including the movement of outlet glaciers. Further, the annual ice layers in glaciers can give information on the climate of long ago and the discovery of an ash layer from a known volcanic eruption is of very great importance for the confirmation of the age determination of the ice layers. Glaciological research actually started in 1919 with the trip of the Swedes, Wadell and Ygberg, mentioned above. Several trips were made onto Vatnajökull in the years 1934–1936 due to the Grímsvötn eruption of 1934. After the foundation of the Iceland Glaciological Society in 1950 the number of trips to Vatnajökull with mechanically driven equipment increased, both for research and for sightseeing purposes. On the map on page 48 the routes of the Society's research expeditions in 1968 and 1969 are shown (JÖRFI 1968, 1969). Grímsvötn are visited every year for measurements, but other routes differ somewhat from year to year. At several places in the Vatnajökull glacier snow pits are dug in the spring down through the layer of snow which has accumulated on that spot during the previous winter. Samples are taken in 30 cm long hollow cylinders from the surface of the pit to the bottom. The snow of each sample is weighed, studied and measured, and part of it is put into plastic containers for subsequent analysis in a laboratory. From the bottom of the snow pit a hand drill is applied for a further penetration into the glacier down to a depth of about 10 m, cores of 40 cm length being taken at a time. These cores are also weighed, its ice layers studied and measured, and samples put into separate containers destined for the laboratory. In the last few years drillings have been made by means of an electrical thermal drill to collect samples from greater depths at Bárðarbunga, where a depth of more than 100 m has been reached. The main purpose of this research work is to study the amount of snow accumulated at various points on the glacier and to determine the amount of its potential melt-water content. This knowledge is of practical value as it indicates the amount of water which can be expected to emerge from the glacier to different rivers, some of which produce electricity in hydro-electric power plants. During the last few years the Science Institute of the University of Iceland has, in co-operation with the Glaciological Society, collected samples of snow from different glaciers in Iceland for the measurement of its deuterium and tritium content. This research has shown that Bárðarbunga (2000 m) can for all practical purposes be considered an arctic glacier in the sense that very little melting takes place there in spite of its being considered a temperate glacier. Therefore, deuterium measurements of ice cores from Bárðarbunga could give information about the climate in Iceland over a period of several centuries. Due to the pressure from the ice masses above, the lower layers are more and more compacted and are therefore thinner. Thus, the bottom ice layers in Bárðarbunga might be 400–1000 years old. It is hoped that deeper drillings there might give information on temperature in Iceland in the past, possibly back to the time of the settlement.

A core drilling through the Greenland ice sheet was completed recently. The deepest part of the core was found to be more than 100,000 years old, and measurements of annual mean temperatures, therefore, cover the same period. These measurements are easier to make on an arctic glacier as almost no melting takes place there. On Icelandic glaciers it is only in winter that the precipitation is snow. During summer it is mostly rain which flows away together with the part of the winter snow that is melted during the warm season.

It is easy enough to keep warm when drilling manually in a snow pit. The temperature of the snow in a pit like this is usually 0°C. near the top, but often it is –1°C to –3°C at a depth of 4–5 m. – But glaciological research also requires many other odd jobs: When staying in a camp for a while, travellers on glaciers often build a toilette of snow for added comfort. The maintenance of the snowmobiles often requires considerable skill.

59

The first explorers of Vatnajökull travelled on foot or on skis, sometimes pulling sledges. Above and below skiers are travelling in the Grímsvötn area because skis are still handy for short explorations although most tours of Vatnajökull today are made by snowmobiles. Crevasses are often found at the foot of the mountains in the Grímsvötn depression, but they are most pronounced, of course, just after a glacier flood has occurred when the water level of the lake has sunk by as much as 200 m.

glacier tracks

In former days travelling over the Icelandic glaciers was either done on foot or on horseback. In addition to crossings by fishermen over Vatnajökull from the north to the fishing stations in the Hornafjörður district, it is also known that the Drangajökull was frequently crossed when the northernmost part of the Western Fjords was still inhabited. Then driftwood was transported across the glacier to the Isafjarðardjúp. – The British explorer, Watts, and his Icelandic guides travelled on foot on Vatnajökull, both in 1874 and 1875, pulling a sledge part of the way. The Dane, Kock, crossed Vatnajökull on horseback in 1912, and the Swedes, Wadell and Ygberg, were also on horseback when they reached Grímsvötn in 1919. The expeditions to the volcanic eruption site at Grímsvötn in 1934–1936 mostly used skis and sledges. The Swedish-Icelandic expedition to Vatnajökull in 1936 used four sledge dogs, and that is the only time dogs have been used for pulling sledges on Icelandic glaciers. Today snowmobiles are practically the only means of transportation used for travelling on Vatnajökull, and usually they pull special sledges loaded with petrol barrels, provisions and equipment. Most of the participants bring with them skiing equipment, which is convenient for shorter trips. To be towed by a snowmobile over the immense expanses of the Vatnajökull glacier makes an effortless, but exhilarating, skiing experience. Melt-water and soft ice can make the first lap below the firn line quite difficult. On the glacier driving by night is the usual procedure when the weather is warm, because then a crust of sufficient strength may be formed on the surface for the snowmobiles to ride more easily. Helicopters and small aircraft have been used for shorter visits to the glaciers.

⇨

Snowmobile tracks seen from the Grímsfjall down to the Grímsvötn depression. The first rays of the morning sun reveal any uneven features on the surface of the firn.

snow into ice

All fresh snow that falls on a glacier, regardless whether it falls as snowflakes or hail, gradually turns into ice. Fresh snow is very light because it contains a lot of air. All snowflakes are made up of hexagonal crystals, but they may vary a great deal in form. Sometimes the arms are formed by a network of long fine needles of ice only, but sometimes they consist of hexagonal flat plates (see picture at top left). When fresh snow falls on the glacier in calm weather, a light surface layer will soon be formed. When the snow drifts, the arms of the snowflakes soon break off and they will melt slightly due to friction and sunshine, if there is any. During night they will often refreeze together with their own melt-water. In this way the snow becomes harder and more granular than fresh snow (see picture middle left), but this surface layer still contains some bubbles of air. When new layers of snow accumulate on top of existing ones, the pressure increases. Melt-water and rain drain down into the lower layers and refreeze there. In this way the snow is compacted by pressure, melting and refreezing into hard, granulated firn, often with ice layers in between (bottom picture left). Deeper down in the glacier the ice increasingly turns into compact ice with greater transparency, but still containing some air bubbles. The picture to the right shows an ice core from a depth of 40 metres on Bárðarbunga, its size having been enlarged by nearly 5 to 1. There are still several air bubbles left in spite of the great pressure above. In the ice caves of Grímsfjall old layers of glacial ice can be seen without drilling. These caves are created by melting in the ice of the hill slope by volcanic heat. The blue colour from the daylight shining through the ceiling is often very beautiful (see p. 64 and 65).

The pictures on this page were all taken with macro lens equipment on 1st and 2nd June 1969 near snow pit No. 5 to the north-west of Esjufjöll. It had been snowing during the night but the frost was only −5°C. Therefore a prompt action was needed on the part of the photographer before each ice crystal melted or evaporated. The ice crystal in the picture at top left is enlarged about 70 times. The picture of freshly fallen snow (the picture in the centre) is enlarged about 10 times and the same applies to the bottom picture of rough firn from a drill-hole through a two-year-old ice layer.

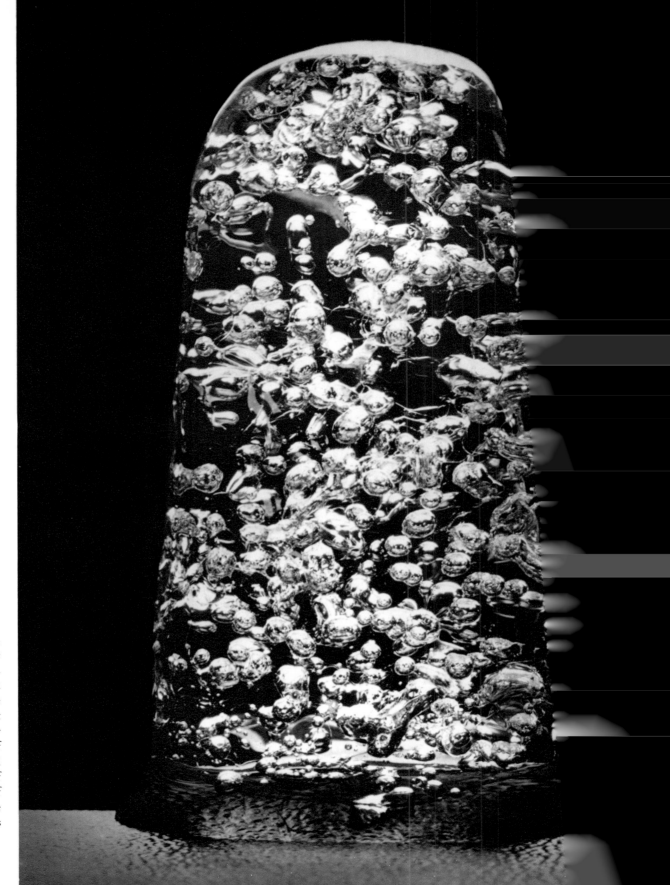

An ice core, enlarged 5 times, from a 40 m deep hole drilled in the Bárðarbunga in Vatnajökull on June 6th 1968. The ice has become glassy under pressure, but it still contains many air bubbles. In 1969 a depth of more than 100 m was reached in Bárðarbunga by means of a thermal drill. At a depth of 101 m an ash layer from the 1918 eruption of Katla was found.

Under the firn covering the slopes of Grímsfjall large ice caves develop owing to the geothermal heat in the sides of the caldera. The entrances to the ice caves, however, are often hidden under a snow cover until the middle of summer. It is pitch-dark down there so that lighting equip-ment is essential. The tuff slope below is very steep and is luke-warm in places. Where daylight penetrates through crevasses in the dome the ice assumes a beautiful blue hue.

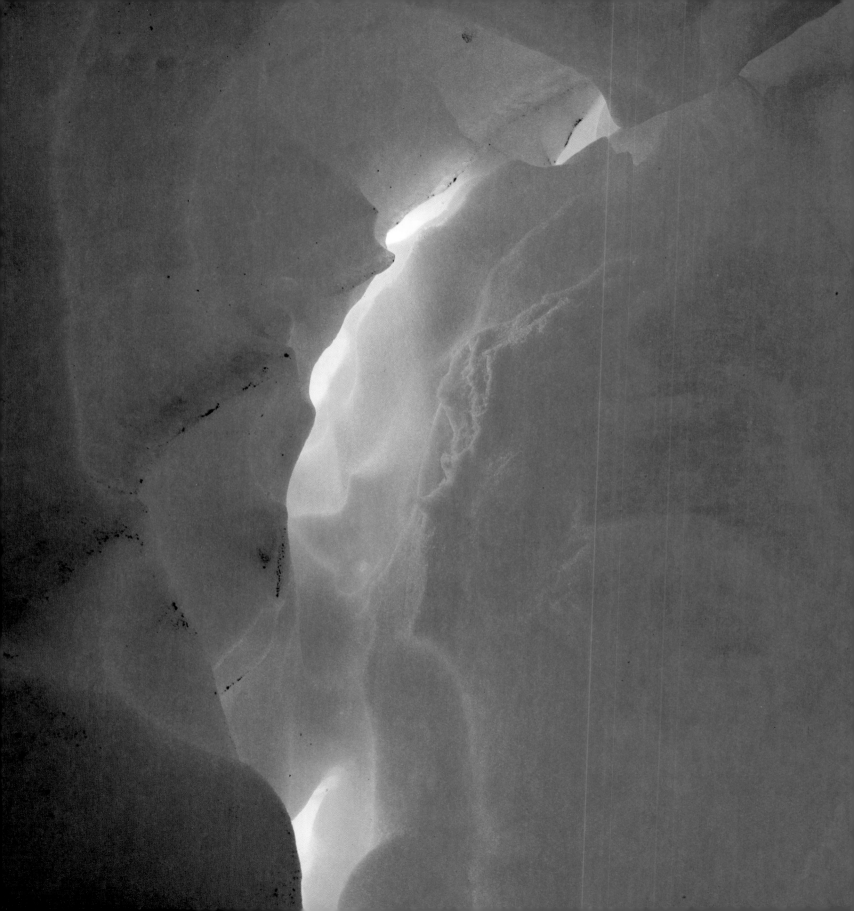

ice surface

The surface of glacier ice may vary enormously because frost, melting by the sun and the wind reshape the snow and the firn on the ice cap in many different ways. The top picture to the left shows an ice surface on the eastern part of the Vatnajökull ice cap. Such crust with ripple marks formed by the sun and the wind covered a considerable area. The lower picture to the left was taken of an ice surface on the very steep sides of the Hvannadalshnjúkur peak. These ice tops are mostly formed by the sun melting the surface and its refreezing. Below is a picture from the thermal ice caves of Grímsfjall where the volcanic heat has unevenly melted the various layers of the ice. The picture to the right was taken in drifting snow. The sharp irregular ridges formed on the snow surface by wind erosion and deposition are called sastrugi. They are parallel to the direction of the wind.

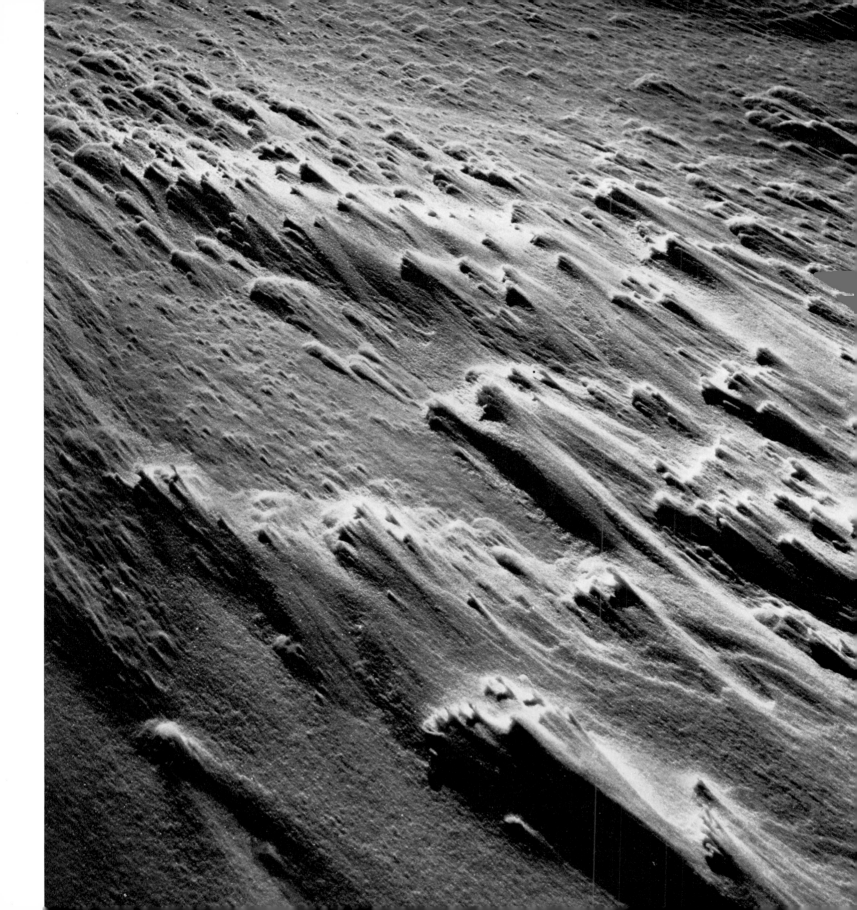

◁ Sunrise on the glacial firn is a breathtaking spectacle: The roseate colours of dawn blend with the bluish hues of the firn in a magnificent ever-changing display. This picture was taken on the eastern part of Vatnajökull on 11th June 1968.

⇧ A view towards Herðubreið from the eastern part of Vatnajökull, facing Brúarjökull. The snowmobile tracks often become circuitous when crevasses have to be by-passed.

Öræfajökull

Although Öræfajökull is connected to the main ice sheet of Vatnajökull, it is really a separate ice cap because it lies on a considerably higher level south of the main glacier. They are connected by an ice ridge, Hermannaskarð (1350 m), on the west side of the nunatak Þuríðartindur (1741 m), and a separate ice cap called Jökulbak (1922 m), which offers an excellent view of Hvannadalshnjúkur (2119 m), the highest peak in Iceland, towering majestically with its ice cover usually right to the top. Then there is Tjaldskarð (1844 m), a narrow snow-covered pass which must be followed with great care because both sides are very steep. Then there is another ice cupola, Snæbreið (2041 m). From it there is a magnificent view of the enormous ice-filled caldera of the volcano Öræfajökull, but many peaks along the edges stand out of the ice, the biggest of these nunataks being Hvannadalshnjúkur (see picture on page 51).

As mentioned before, the physician and naturalist Sveinn Pálsson was the first to climb Öræfajökull. His ascent is reported in his treatise on glaciology. He started from the farm Kvískerjar on the 11th August 1794 and climbed a peak in the south-east part of the glacier together with one of his companions. According to his measurements of the altitude and his description of the ascent the peak in question is considered to have been Knappur (1927 m). From there it is about four km across the caldera to Hvannadalshnjúkur. The first to climb the latter peak were the Norwegian Hans Frisak in 1813 and the English-

The picture above shows Hvannadalshnjúkur, bathed in the morning sun, as it looks from Snæbreið (2041 m), which is still throwing a shadow right to its foot. – Below the whole crew of the snowmobile Gosi are having dinner at a camp on the top of Snæbreið on a calm and sunny day. Even the photographer can be spotted in the snowmobile mirror together with Hvannadalshnjúkur in the background. – Below to the right a snowmobile is leaving Hermannaskarð for a climb on to Öræfajökull. In the background Þuríðartindur is to the right and Esjufjöll to the left.

Hvannadalshnjúkur takes on varying forms, depending on the degree of daylight. A majestic sight is the background of this camp at the foot of the highest peak in Iceland which now has put on its finest garb in the midday sun. The easiest route from the camp to the top is across the ridge to the right, past the rock-face, and then askew up the moun-tain side where it desappears behind the summit. The route is very steep and the snow is usually very hard. The summit is a rather small snow cap, often very icy. It goes without saying that in good visibility the view from Hvannadalshnjúkur in all directions is beyond descrip-tion.

71

man Fr. W. W. Howell in 1891. The best direct route to the Hvannadalshnjúkur, apart from the snowmobile route described above, is from the farm Sandfell in Öræfi. From the ice cap Snæbreið snowmobiles can be driven right down to the foot of Hvannadalshnjúkur, where there is an excellent place for camping (see picture on page 71). The height of the peak from its foot is less than 250 m, but it is very steep and great care is needed due to crevasses and glassy ice. Hvannadalshnjúkur can vary a great deal in appearance as the light changes. But somehow the feeling of supreme grandeur is most pronounced when the last rays of the setting sun colour its ice-covered peak in gold

while the surrounding ice surface below is submerged in dark blue shadows. In clear weather there is, of course, a breathtaking view in all directions, but often the 'lowland' below the 1000 m altitude level is overclouded, even if the glacier to the north is completely clear. The border mountains Hrútafjallstindar and Skaftafellsfjöll with the Þumall (The Thumb), a pinnacle of basalt, tower against the ice cap, whereas the nunataks Þórðarhyrna and Grímsfjall can be seen farther away. The Skeiðarárjökull and Lómagnúpur to the west and the coastline to Hornafjörður to the east can be seen in clear weather. North over the Vatnajökull the Kverkfjöll, Herðubreið and Snæfell mountains are

Above is a view from Hvannadalshnjúkur to the north-west over Vatnajökull. Hrútfjallstindar are nearest, but farther away, near the edge of the glacier, are the Skaftafell mountains, where the rock Þumall and Miðfellstindur peak may be seen. Over Skaftafellsjökull and Morsárdalur there is a cloud cover, only the highest peaks penetrating it. On the other hand, the sky is clear over Vatnajökull where Þórðarhyrna, Háabunga and Grímsfjall can be seen.

Here the last rays of the setting sun gild Hvannadalshnjúkur which towers above the dark-blue ice-cap. Some travellers can be seen standing on the summit, but in the blue haze further below part of the Öræfajökull caldera can be faintly discerned.

visible in the distance. Close to Hvannadalshnjúkur there is a magnificent view of the roughly crevassed outlet glacier Svínafellsjökull and the peculiar mountain ridge Kirkjan ('The Church') an appropriate name because of its shape and many towers.—Iceland's highest peak has not always been peaceful. Öræfajökull is actually the biggest existing volcano in Iceland, both in height and volume. Its volume is three times that of Snæfellsjökull, and Öræfajökull is the third in height among European volcanoes. Since the settlement it has erupted only twice, however, both eruptions being most spectacular. The first eruption of Öræfajökull in historical times was in 1362 and was one of the biggest explosive eruptions known to have occurred in the world in historical times. In this eruption a whole settlement of 30–40 farms was completely destroyed, and temporarily all the inhabited area in the vicinity of Öræfajökull is believed to have been abandoned. In his treatise Sveinn Pálsson writes

◁

This peculiar mountain ridge just below Hvannadalshnjúkur is called Kirkjan ('The Church'), quite an appropriate name, because it is adorned with a number of spires. Here a mass of clouds suddenly ascends Öræfajökull from the lower level of Svínafellsjökull. The picture was taken on the top of Snæbreið (2041 m) just before Kirkjan disappeared into the clouds.

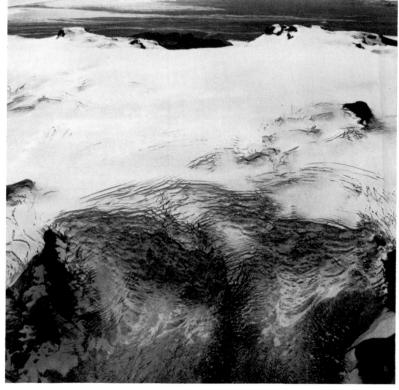

⇨

To the right there is an aerial view of Öræfajökull from the east. Hvannadalshnjúkur is farthest to the left and is seen against Skeiðarársandur in the background. At the beginning of the outlet glacier the crevasses widen and increase in number as the slope gets steeper, speeding up the movement of the ice. The picture on the next page (p. 75) is an aerial view over Skeiðarárjökull to Öræfajökull from the west. Nearest is the snout of the Skeiðarárjökull outlet glacier where it extends down on to Skeiðarársandur, then the Skaftafell mountains and Morsárdalur. The river Skeiðará emerges from under a corner of Skeiðarárjökull and flows right across the Morsárdalur where it is joined by the river Morsá close to the farm of Skaftafell. The next outlet glaciers are Skaftafellsjökull and Svínafellsjökull, and between them Hafrafell. Hvannadalshnjúkur towers against the sky, but down below to the left is the black ridge Kirkjan, emerging from the glacier. The farm Svínafell is at the snout of Svínafellsjökull.

When the first morning sun bathes the wide expanses of the Vatnajökull firn in its profusion of rays, a myriad of ice crystals glisten all over the glacier. There is nothing like it, except perhaps an aerial view of an illuminated city where thousands of lights twinkle continuously. This phenomenon cannot be seen when the sun is low in the evening or in the morning if the air is warm. In the picture to the right there is a view from Snæbreið over Breiðamerkurjökull to Veðurárdalsfjöll.

76

that the following had been reported on the destruction that occurred in 1362: 'One morning about milking-time at the farm of Svínafell a shepherd named Hallur and some milkmaids heard a thundering crash from the glacier just above the farm. They all got panic-stricken, but shortly afterwards there was another crash even more powerful. Then the shepherd is reported to have said that it would not be wise to wait for the third one and without further ado he took to his heels to the mountain above and reached a cave, still called Flosahellir, not far away from the farm. Then came the third crash, and at the same moment the glacier exploded with enormous noise. Water and ice filled every ravine in the mountain and washed away all the people and the livestock in the settlement below or buried them all in deep mud, sand and glacial debris inside the farmhouses, with the exception of the shepherd...' During this eruption very large amounts of rhyolite-tephra burst out of the volcano. It has been estimated that it could have covered the whole country with a 10 cm thick layer, but fortunately most of this tephra fell in the sea. The second eruption of Öræfajökull started on 4th August 1727 with two strong earthquakes. Then two outlet glaciers advanced,

suddenly, covering the lowlands with mud and ice. We are told that tephra and volcanic bombs fell continuously for three days, darkening the sky. The eruption continued until 25th May 1728. This second eruption was, however, not as violent as the first, and since then there have been no signs of the fire beneath the ice cover of Öræfajökull.

⇑
Breiðamerkurjökull is one of the Icelandic outlet glaciers which dip their snouts into a glacier lake where icebergs break off for a free ride on the water. The black stripes on the glacier, lateral and medial moraines, come into being when the moving ice of an outlet glacier is divided by an opposing nunatak and reunited below it. The moraines consist of stones and clay eroded by the outlet glacier from the mountain sides and transported down to the lowlands. On Breiðamerkurjökull these moraines are derived from Esjufjöll and Máfabyggðir, showing quite clearly the direction of the ice movement.

The ice floes on the Breiðamerkur glacier lake are not all big, but they vary a great deal in shape and colour. In their travel across the lake they often hit the bottom, melt and break up until they are small enough for the river Jökulsá á Breiðamerkursandi to bring down to the sea.

glacier lakes

There are two types of glacier lakes that are created or maintained by glaciers, apart from ones caused by the effects of volcanic heat as in the case of Grímsvötn (see page 54). Glacier lakes are often formed at the snout of outlet glaciers when they retreat due to ameliorating climate. Over a long period of time an outlet glacier builds up an end moraine, but it also buries its snout considerably deeper into the ground above the moraine. When it has withdrawn further a glacier lake is left in the depression, and the melt-water that has accumulated in the lake will find its way through the lowest part of the moraine to the sea, forming a glacial river. All this is illustrated in the picture on page 81, showing the snout of the outlet glacier Fjalljökull, a part of Öræfajökull, reaching into the glacier lake Fjallsárlón. The foot of the Breiðamerkurjökull once reached much further towards the beach than it does now. There was no glacier lake there then, but the Jökulsá á Breiðamerkursandi, the shortest big river in Iceland, came straight out from under the foot of the glacier, crossing the narrow sand beach and flowing direct into the Atlantic Ocean. Now there is a big and deep glacier lake at the end of the outlet glacier with enormous icebergs breaking off the snout and floating on the glacier lake as shown in the pictures on pages 78, 79 and 80. When the naturalist Þorvaldur Thoroddsen crossed Breiðamerkursandur in 1894, the distance from the glacier's edge to the sea-shore was only 256 m and heavy seas carried driftwood right up to the glacier. Breiðamerkurjökull is the only Icelandic glacier which has been so close to the sea. The glacial river Jökulsá á Breiðamerkursandi was then deemed to be the most difficult one to cross south of Vatnajökull, and it was

A view of the Breiðamerkursandur glacier lake. Ærfjall is to the left and Breiðamerkurfjall to the right, but between them is Fjallsjökull, an outlet glacier extending from Öræfajökull. The farm Fjall was situated near the foot of Breiðamerkurjökull from about 900 A.D. until it was buried under the glacier in the years between 1695 and 1709. Now its site has returned as the glacier retired. – Many of the ice floes in the Breiðamerkursandur lake are of peculiar shapes.

⇨

This aerial view of the snout of Fjallsjökull to the east of Öræfajökull reveals many rows of old moraines. The Fjallsá lake collects the melt-water, which then proceeds to the sea. The works of man look tiny in comparison with those of nature. Just below the lake there is a fairly big bridge, barely visible, the picture being taken from a considerable height.

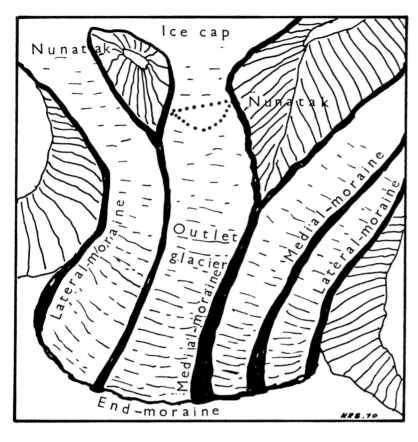

frequently by-passed by crossing the glacier snout. Now motor vehicles can cross this river by a suspension bridge just below the glacier lake. In the picture of Breiðamerkurjökull on page 78 several medial moraines are visible. These are ridges of rock debris that were eroded by the glacier from both sides of nunataks as it passed. Immediately below the nunataks these ridges of debris from each nunatak are re-united in one medial moraine. At Breiðamerkurjökull these medial moraines come from Esjufjöll and Máfabyggðir (see map on page 48). The drawing on the left shows how medial moraines and lateral moraines are formed, the latter occurring along the sides of an outlet glacier. On the drawing the dots on the outlet glacier between the nunataks indicate the moving speed at different points across its ice stream. Marks put in a straight line across it will after a reasonable time be found at the places indicated, showing the relative speed of different parts of a cross section of the stream. The greatest speed is in the middle, whereas it is much slower on both sides. The medial moraines also show very clearly the direction of movement in the outlet glaciers, as can be seen on the aerial views of Skeiðarárjökull illustrated here. In the top left hand corner of both these pictures is the lake Grænalón, a good specimen of the second type of glacier lakes. The Grænalón is an ice-dammed lake. It was formed in a valley by the side of the glacier-filled Skeiðarárdalur valley. The water in this lake consists only of melt-water from the glacier as there is no volcanic heat here. The water level in Grænalón rises until the water can either overflow the glacier dam or, what happens quite frequently when the water level exceeds nine tenths of the thickness of the edge of the outlet glacier damming up the lake, the water lifts the glacier edge and the lake is emptied by means of a sudden glacier burst below the glacier down into the river Súla. For a long time these glacier bursts remained a mystery.

⇦

The lateral and medial moraines of Skeiðarárjökull clearly show the direction of its movement. In the top left-hand corner of the picture the outlet glacier closes a side-valley where Grænalón ('Green Lake') is formed between Grænafjall close to the glacier and Mt. Eggjar.

The nature of Grænalón remained a mystery for a long time, but it is an ice-dammed lake which intermittently causes glacier floods in the river Súla. At one time Grænalón was identified with Grímsvötn because volcanic or geothermal heat was thought to be the cause of these glacier floods, and it was even thought that the glacier floods in the river Skeiðará originated in it before the connection between Skeiðarárdalur and Grímsvötn became evident. The surface level of Grænalón used to be at a height of 620 m, being drained by the River Núpsá when the level of the lake was at a maximum. Since then Skeiðarárjökull has shrunk in the area where it dams up the lake. Therefore, the water level of the lake has subsided so that none of the water finds its way to the Núpsá. On the other hand, the lake is emptied under the edge of the glacier at intervals of a few years, or is drained to some extent by a brook that flows along the edge of the glacier near Eggjar and Eystrafjall, which is to the left in this picture below Grænalón. The Vatnajökull ice-cap is in the back-ground.

winter snow

The winter snow comes to all of us who live in northerly countries without our having to look for it in the mountains or on glaciers. Those who are fond of skiing welcome the winter snow and young people accustomed to winter sports from their childhood will always remember the delight and freedom of the wide expanses where everything is clean and white and any direction offers a possible route. Then there is the silence of the wilderness. Explorers of the Polar wastes have described the immense snowfields there as 'the great white silence', but even in the skiing areas of inhabited countries it is possible for members of a small party of skiers to experience this silence of the wide expanses. A young man's skiing experience on a clear and frosty mid-winter night will long be remembered – the whole sky being completely covered with the amber-green flashing folds of the northern lights, and the soft and gentle

carpet of snow reflecting the green hue of the sky, mingling with the blue shadows in the snow. Even the most romantic description of such a night will never do justice to the fascination burned into one's mind for a whole lifetime, although in actual fact it can undeniably be a costly nuisance both for individuals and the community at large. The snow can disrupt communications and impede work in general, prevent the use of pasture in winter and cause damage to property. Anyhow, the winter snow is an annual visitor on every farm and in every town in northerly countries. Therefore, we might as well be prepared for its arrival and fully enjoy its beauty and charm. In Iceland and other Nordic countries skis were first used as a means of transportation between farms and villages when the winter snow covered all the land. This use of skis is no less important today for nature lovers, although motor-driven means of transport on land and in the air have firmly established themselves for all practical purposes. Ski-walking with camping equipment for travel in the mountains in late winter or early spring can be refreshing and exhilarating, and in many ways the mountains look quite different from their summer garb when they are covered with winter snow. It is often like looking at a different landscape altogether. That is how it is with Botnssúlur, the peaks at the bottom of Hvalfjörður to the north of Þingvellir. Skis are of little use for climbing here, however, due to the steepness of the mountain slopes. The highest peak is 1095 m, and the others are not much lower. Botnssúlur are free from snow in summer, except that some snow patches on the northern slopes may not melt every year. In winter the snow covers these peaks with an attractive mantle which is never exactly the same because the snow is as changeable as the winter fashion. The layers of snow vary with the wind, and icing on the rocks depends on the interaction of frost, sunshine and the wind.

Often the winter snow brings out the main contours of the landscape. It covers up the details, but shows up the

Botnssúlur is the name of a few mountain peaks at the bottom end of Hvalfjörður. They are in a northerly direction from Þingvellir. The highest peak is 1095 m, but they are all more or less of the same height. These pictures were taken while the winter snow cover still remained on April 9th. In summer Botnssúlur are free of snow, except for a few snow patches that often linger in hollows on the slopes.

characteristic landscape features. This is particularly true when a thin layer of snow covers mountain views as in these pictures, which also illustrate the formation of three parts of Iceland: The West, North, and East parts of Iceland are built up of basalt layers from old volcanic eruptions. Originally these lava layers were nearly horizontal, forming a massive plateau, at least 5000 m thick. Later this plateau broke into smaller parts, sinking and rising along faults and inclining mainly towards the centre of the country. There deep faults opened down to the liquid magma below, and lava flow and tephra filled up the centre of Iceland. In the older basalt areas of the country the wind, water and the glaciers took their turn at chiselling out the landscape. The rivers followed the fissures and made them deeper. The outlet glaciers made the steep-sided valleys wider and deeper. Later the sea invaded the glacier-eroded coastal valleys, and fjords came into being. If the landscape shown in these pictures is studied with its development in mind, it is relatively easy to visualize how fissures, hanging valleys, valleys and mountain ridges were created because here the winter snow has exaggerated the most prominent features.

The winter snow sometimes reveals the erosion caused by water and valley-glaciers, as can be seen in these three pictures which are from different parts of Iceland. At the top left are the mountains of the north-west peninsula with a view over Arnarfjörður. Below it to the left are mountains in East Iceland with Dyrfjöll in the background, and above is a picture of the very rugged mountain chain between Skagafjörður and Eyjafjörður in the North. All the pictures quite clearly show the erosive effects of water and the outlet glaciers of the ice age on basalt lava layers, piled one on top of the other.

87

The winter snow can vary in form in very much the same way as glacial ice. Above there are peculiar stripes, caused by the wind, in a ravine in Mt. Eggjar near Grænalón.

Even in lowland lava near inhabited areas winter snow may be endowed with purity and beauty of both shape and form when the low winter sun brings out clearly every irregularity by means of sharp shadows.

88

Every skier looks with delight forward to the advent of the winter snow. This is a view from the ski-slopes of Seljalandsdalur near Ísafjörður over to the mountains at the bottom of the fjord.

Icicles are formed when water trickles down in frostly weather as it does in this picture of a sea-cliff. The water seeps out between the rock layers, forming the icicles which gradually grow longer and thicker as the descending water freezes. Ultimately they reach right down to the beach and form ice columns which gradually grow thicker and join other icicles, resulting in a glassy ice-wall which looks like a frozen waterfall.

icing

Icing may be of many different kinds due to differences in outer conditions. Icicles are formed where dripping water freezes. They are common both in nature and on house-eaves. Hoarfrost in the form of feathers and fans on window glass is also well known. Icing can, of course, be formed on any exposed object. Rime on trees is of outstanding beauty, especially in the first rays of the morning sun. When frost arrives suddenly in autumn, very beautiful rime formations can often be observed on the moss of lavafields, particularly near openings in the lava. Thick lava streams are often very porous, containing a considerable amount of warm and humid air in the autumn. When the temperature falls below freezing point, this air flows out through the openings where condensation of its humidity takes place with the result that the surrounding moss looks as if it were covered with exotic white flowers. They are, however, very fine leaves of hoarfrost, consisting of a number of ice needles which glitter when they are caught by the winter sun. Near hot springs where warm vapour drizzles over the immediate vicinity, there are very interesting icing formations on plants when the vapour freezes.

The cave Raufarhólshellir is remarkable at any time of the year, but in early spring and in winter when the snow does not prevent its accessibility, interesting ice formations can be studied there. Besides the icicles hanging down from the ceiling, ice pillars (stalagmites) rise from the floor where the water dripping from the icicles has frozen. The whole floor near the entrance of the cave is covered with slippery ice, so crampons are advisable, but this fairy-tale world is certainly worth a visit. Deeper in the cave there is total darkness so that good lighting is essential.

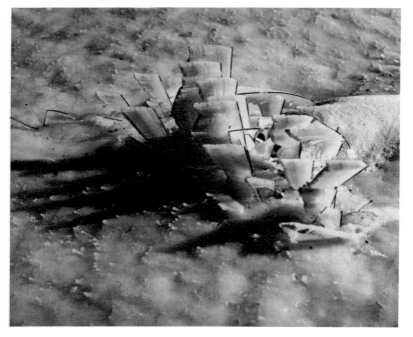

In many places icing is the result of warm or humid air coming in contact with solid objects in frosty weather. Above there are fine hoarfrost formations that look like the petals of flowers. This hoarfrost was formed on lava moss. The picture to the left shows ice-covered straws near a geyser. Steam and hot water is emitted by the hot spring and the moisture freezes on the straws which the wind turns into ice plates. – The picture to the right was taken in the Raufarhólshellir ('Raufarhóll Cave') in winter. Icicles hang from the ceiling, stretching towards their counterparts, the stalagmites, which rise from the floor where the water-drops from the icicles freeze as well.

ice-bound water

The winter alters the appearance of the waterfalls. The Gullfoss is generally thought to be one of the most beautiful waterfalls in Iceland and it is best known as shown in the small picture to the right below. But the winter garb of the Gullfoss is no less attractive. After some days of frost in the highlands the Gullfoss canyon was looking as it is shown in the picture to the left, taken in about 20 °C. below freezing point on 31st March 1968. The waterfall itself was not frozen, but the spray from it had accumulated on the rocks of the canyon just as on any other opposing object. Quick action was needed for the photographic work as the camera lens had to be de-iced just before each exposure.

The picture above is a view down the Gullfoss canyon. It gives a rather chilly feeling, at least to those who remember the green grass-fields on the banks of the canyon in summer. However, the ice has its charm, too, and the north wind blowing from the Langjökull glacier towards the Gullfoss on a frosty winter day is invigorating enough.

Small brooks are also worth seeing in their winter costume. Even if the water in rivulets is not completely frozen, the banks and surrounding areas accumulate ice from its spray. But with the coming of spring the ice soon melts, and with its disappearance the first buds arrive on the scene and there is life in the soil once again.

hot springs under ice

In many places in Iceland hot springs are to be found under ice, where they sometimes create huge ice caves by melting the covering snow. Among well known such places is the north-west slopes of Mt. Hrafntinnusker near Landmannalaugar, east of Hekla. Hrafntinnusker is 1080 m high. It does not have a permanent ice cap, only snow or ice patches on its slopes. If there are hot springs under the firn, crevasses develop in the ice cover with ice caves underneath. Even if there are hot springs on the floors of the caves, it is easy enough to walk into them, but inside there is high humidity, both due to the steam from the hot springs and

water dripping from the ceiling above. From the outside it is easy to see how the firn has been gently sinking due to the heat underneath as the yearly ice layers in the firn have bent above the openings into the caves. This shows the flexibility of glacier ice. It can easily bend if its movement is slow enough. On the other hand, it is brittle and will easily break if it is subjected to sudden and powerful stresses, resulting in the formation of crevasses. Sometimes, therefore, part of the ceiling of an ice cave tumbles down so that great care is advisable on the part of any would-be explorers. Due to the melting of the ceiling a most peculiar bowl-like surface is formed with ice tops and ridges in between. These formations can be seen in the picture above although it is somewhat marred by steam and vapour which make photography rather difficult.

On the slopes of Hrafntinnusker near Landmannalaugar there is glacial firn even though there is no ice cap on the mountain peak. But in these slopes there are also hot springs which melt deep ice caves in the firn. This picture clearly shows the plastic nature of glacial ice which can shrink and bend if the movement is slow enough, whereas it will crack or break if it is subjected to sudden stresses.

water

Water appears in so many forms that it has actually been discussed in every chapter of this book so far. Sea ice, glaciers, winter snow and icing consist of water in one form or another, and so does the steam from the hot springs. Let us now have a look at plain cold water as it is found in lakes and rivers. – The climate is a dominant factor in the nature of every country because on it depends the development of the soil, the vegetation and animal life to a large extent. The most important factors of the climate of each place are temperature, precipitation, sunshine and the wind. The precipitation is, of course, very important for the growth of all vegetation and for the water balance of the land. The annual precipitation is 400–600 mm in Northern Iceland,

but 1000–4000 mm in the South. It is by far the biggest on the southern slopes of Vatnajökull and Mýrdalsjökull and considerably lower just north of these glaciers. Due to climatic reasons rivers are divided into mountain rivers and glacier-melt rivers. Mountain rivers are in turn either direct run-off rivers or spring-fed rivers. Direct run-off rivers drain surface water from the mountains in the Tertiary basaltic areas, and therefore these rivers swell rapidly during rainy periods, but almost dry up in dry and frosty weather. Spring-fed rivers are also mountain rivers, but their sources are springs, the water of which has often come considerable distances underground. Therefore, the discharge of water in spring-fed rivers is much more constant, any appreciable fluctuations extending over relatively long periods. Some of Iceland's biggest rivers are combinations of all three types. That is, for instance, the case of the river Hvítá in Borgarfjörður. The land drained by a river is called a river basin or drainage area. The biggest river basins in Iceland are drained by the following rivers: The Jökulsá á Fjöllum (7950 km^2), the Þjórsá (7530 km^2), the Ölfusá (6100 km^2), the Skjálfandafljót (3860 km^2), and the Héraðsvötn (3650 km^2). The waterfall Goðafoss is in the river Skjálfandafljót, which like the Hvítá in Borgarfjörður is all in one: a direct run-off river, a spring-fed river, and a glacier-melt river. When the weather has been frosty for some time, there is very little surface water in it, but in heavy rain the river can swell rapidly for a short time. The spring-fed water in the Skjálfandafljót comes mainly from the Ódáðahraun lava desert, and in winter most of the water has its origin there. Of the total water flow the glacier melt-water forms only a relatively small part, although in summer it increases con-

Fjallfoss in the river Dynjandi (the waterfall itself is also often called Dynjandi) does not contain much water, but it is beautifully shaped. Goðafoss, on the other hand, plunges down with enormous force, consisting of both glacial water and surface or spring water as the drainage area of the Skjálfandafljót is very large, extending almost as far as Bárðarbunga in the Vatnajökull glacier.

A small waterfall in a nameless clear mountain rivulet may be a beautiful sight in its modesty. The bog moss assumes a light-green colour because it has a penchant for moisture. Many a weary traveller is glad to bend down to a small brook and to quench his thirst in the cool and fresh water.

siderably. So far only a small amount of available water power in Iceland has been harnessed, but measurements of the water flow in most of the biggest rivers are taken continually all the year round in preparation of hydro-electric projects.

But water is also essential for growth, and although the big waterfalls are certainly impressive spectacles, a small nameless rivulet in the mountains may present us with idyllic loveliness that is no less enchanting.

Now that the Jökulfirðir ('Glacier Fjords') of the North-West peninsula have been rid of livestock for many years, knee-high wild flowers grow there in the shelter of the mountains and the glacier.

100

Kverkfjöll

Between the outlet glaciers Dyngjujökull and Brúarjökull a huge mountain area, Kverkfjöll (see map on page 48) divides the northern edge of Vatnajökull. The name owes its origin to Kverkin ('the Throat', see picture on page 103), a great chasm which separates the mountain area in question into two parts, east and west Kverkfjöll. Kverkin is actually part of an old volcanic crater, which has been deformed by a long and narrow outlet glacier, Kverkjökull. Towering on both sides of this outlet glacier there are 1800 m high mountain ridges, but the highest peak in Kverkfjöll is 1920 m. This group of mountains is volcanic, and doubtless the western Kverkfjöll is still an active volcano. Here is one of the biggest thermal areas in Iceland with big steam and hot water springs and boiling mud pots, mainly in, and close by, the Hveradalur, a cleft valley lying in the direction NE to SW. This hot spring valley is in itself one of the most remarkable natural phenomena in Iceland. It is completely covered with hot springs of different types and sizes, steam springs and mud pots, and the slopes on both sides are also boiling to a greater or lesser extent. At the south-west end of the valley there is a glacier-dammed lake, sometimes covered by ice, but sometimes studded with odd icebergs that have broken off the glacier above. There seem to be hot water outlets at the bottom of the lake, but hot water also runs from the springs on the slopes. The hot springs even extend southwards and eastwards underneath the glacier ice where high columns of steam ascend through melted holes in the firn. In other places there are cauldrons in the glacier, formed by the hot springs underneath although they have not melted a hole in the ice above. In a way this place is a small scale model of the Grímsvötn area: an ice-dammed lake, hot springs below, an ice-cover or ice-bergs floating on the water, which is emptied at intervals. To the east of the lake, there are tuff hills with countless boiling springs, and where the end of the hillside meets the glacier, the hot springs have melted the ice around (see picture on page 102).

Northwards, along the tuff ridge on the western side of the Hveradalur, the valley first gets wider and then slopes somewhat upwards. At the north-east end of the lake there is a gentle slope down to the bottom of the valley, which is about 1600 m above sea level. In the valley there are some blue boiling mud pots, sulpurous hot springs, most of them seething with a mass of bubbles. Some of these mud pots are also to be found up on the valley slopes to the east (see picture on page 105). From the end of the lake the valley slopes somewhat up towards a thin ridge across the valley, almost closing it, with small peaks on both sides. North-east of this ridge the valley is completely different in character, now getting V-shaped and much deeper like a cleft, but it opens out further north. The west side of the valley is very steep here, and the colours are extremely rich and varied, even for colourful Iceland. The hot springs are close to each other, covering the whole slope down to the bottom of the valley. The whole area seems to be on the boil as it is thick-set with steam jets (see picture on page 106). To reach this valley slope the easiest way is to follow the ridge on the west side of the valley, because from it there is a splendid view southwards over this fantastic landscape. Along the ridge pillars of rocks that look like petrified giants jut out of the steam, and when the wind occasionally wafts it away, the white ice cap of Vatnajökull can

be seen in the background. Few places in Iceland convey the feeling of contrast between ice and fire as powerfully as this area although several others have frost and fire locked in constant combat, and the colours here are beyond description. On the other hand, there are not many places more remote than Kverkfjöll. From the north there is a long way over lava, sandur-plains and glacial rivers, and from the south the biggest ice cap in the country has to be crossed to reach it. That is the easiest way, however, if the means of transportation are snowmobiles.

It was mentioned above that Kverkfjöll are considered an active volcanic area, and they have often been associated with 'jökulhlaup' (glacier floods) in the rivers that drain melt-water from the northern part of Vatnajökull. Although an eruption in the Hveradalur close to the glacier is not likely to cause a glacier flood since the amount of ice melted would not be substantial so close to the glacier's edge, it is almost certain that the volcanic and hot spring area continues a long way up into the region now covered by the glacier as is indicated by the numerous ice cauldrons. It is considered more likely that the volcanic eruptions which have caused the biggest glacier floods in the river Jökulsá á Fjöllum occurred either in the depression south of the Kverkjökull outlet glacier or in an area by the Dyngjujökull to the north of the Kverkfjöll ridge where it extends farthest into the glacier. This place is on a line with Grímsvötn-Geirvörtur. Eruptions are mentioned in connection with glacier floods in the Jökulsá in 1684, 1716, 1717, and 1726. They may have taken place in this area, or on the ridge between Grímsvötn and the Dyngjujökull area because in 1684 there were glacier floods simultaneously in the Skeiðará and the Jökulsá á Fjöllum.

◁

The Hveradalur valley of the Kverkfjöll in the northern part of Vatnajökull is a meeting-place of heat and cold, boiling hot springs and glacial firn side by side or interlocked. The mountain ridge to the east of Hveradalur is thickly set with steam springs, some of which are underneath the firn, through which they melt holes right to the surface. At the bottom of the picture is a glacier-dammed lake in the Hveradalur. In the bottom of the lake there are hot springs which usually keep parts of the surface free of ice.

△

Above is Kverkin, from which the Kverkfjöll mountains have received their name. The Kverkfjöll are old volcanoes, still containing a great deal of geothermal heat in many places, particularly in the western part of the mountains. Kverkin itself is part of an old crater which the Kverkjökull outlet glacier has penetrated on its way northwards from the Vatnajökull ice cap.

On a spring night there is a beautiful view from Vatnajökull to the
north over the west part of Kverkfjöll and the Hveradalur. The steam
springs melt away the ice at the top end of the Hveradalur, forming
huge ice-cauldrons in the glacier where the ice has been softened by
the subterranean heat. In the background to the left are the Dyngjufjöll
mountains with the volcano Askja which last time erupted in 1961. The
peculiar table mountain Herðubreið on the Mývatnsöræfi is in the
background to the right. The sides of table mountains are steep and
there is a precipitous rock wall around the top, which in turn is either
flat or slightly conical.

⇨

To the north of the lake in the southern part of the Hveradalur in the
Kverkfjöll area there is a number of boiling mud pots (solfataras) in
very colourful surroundings. To the north of this area the valley is
rather shallow, rising gradually to a thin cross-ridge which practically
divides the valley in two dissimilar parts, but to the north of this ridge
the valley is much deeper with very steep mountain slopes, particularly on the west side (see picture on p. 106).

rhyolite

Rhyolite is a fine-textured volcanic rock, composed mostly of quarts (silicon dioxide) and feldspar. It is of many different colours: It can be yellow, pink, reddish, grey-blue and green. There is even a black glassy variety, hrafntinna (obsidian), formed by the rapid cooling of rhyolite magma, mainly on the surface of rhyolite lava-fields, which, however, are very uncommon in Iceland. It is no wonder, therefore, that this multicoloured rock attracts the attention of travellers, even from the distance. When mountain tops consist of rhyolite, they often look as if they were bathed in sunshine even if the sky is overcast. The difference between the mineral composition of basaltic lava and rhyolite is that the silicon content of rhyolite is higher than in basalt. In point of fact, the same Icelandic volcanoes sometimes produce basalt, sometimes intermediate material, and sometimes rhyolite. It has been shown by recent research that the silicium proportion of the magma issuing from some volcanoes increases proportionately to the length of the time that passes between eruptions. When the time between two eruptions is short, the eruption material mainly consists of basaltic lava, but when several centuries elapse between eruptions, explosive eruptions are more likely, producing mainly rhyolite tephra. For example, the volcano Askja erupted rhyolite in 1875, but basalt in 1961, and Snæfellsjökull (see p. 42–45) has erupted rhyolite at least twice. The reason is believed to be that there are separate pockets of magma at a depth of only a few km, although this magma owes its origin to a common source. At the top of such magma pockets lighter materials like silica concentrate when a long time elapses between eruptions, and the next eruption will be an acid-explosive one due to gases released through cooling.

The Torfajökull area is rich in rhyolite formations. The top picture was taken to the south-west of the Landmannalaugar, but the lower picture was taken in the slightly acid Námshraun lava with a view across the river Námskvísl to Suðurnámur.

⇦

This is the west side of the northern part of the Hveradalur valley in the Kverkfjöll area, all dotted with steamy hot springs. Jagged rocks decorate the edge of the slope, which, however, provides the shortest route to the place where the best view is to be had over this unusually colourful area.

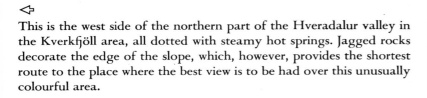

fumaroles

It was mentioned before that in the volcanic parts of Iceland there are 15 high temperature or steam areas. The high temperature areas also contain hot springs, often including the spouting type and steam vents, especially on high ground, which sometimes develop into mud pots, also called fumaroles or solfataras. It is interesting to note that the temperature in the hot springs is apparently highest where rhyolite is the main rock and therefore these areas seem to have some connection with rhyolite eruptions. If a steam spring area has a very high temperature, it can almost invariably be linked with a recent volcanic activity.

In the night before the 17th of May 1724 the 'Mývatn Fires' started with a great explosion on the slopes of Mt. Krafla, northeast of Lake Mývatn, and a new crater, called Víti ('Hell') was formed. After the volcanic eruption finished, the crater was an impressive fumarole, i.e. a boiling mud pot, for more than a whole century. Then it slowly lost its power, and today it is only a big water-filled basin, now called Stóra Víti ('Big Hell'). Now there is another big fumarole, called Litla Víti ('Little Hell') in the bottom of a ravine near by. This mud pot has built up a cone around the hole where the blue mud is boiling. The whole area around this ravine is very colourful, and several openings of older hot springs and dried out mud pots show how the hot spring activity moves around as old mud pots disappear and new ones come into being. A similar area with boiling mud pots and steam jets spouting high into the air is situated east of Námafjall, due east of Mývatn. Also there the blue mud boils in large and small pits. In some the liquid is thin, but in others it is in the form of a thick paste (see page 110).

Above is the colourful side of the Krafla ravine, just below the mud pot Litla Víti. The picture below is of a dried-out clay area with small mud pot holes still boiling underneath.

This large mud pot in the lower part of the Krafla ravine is called Litla Víti ('Little Hell'). The blue clay boils and bubbles in a cone-shaped crater, built up by the mud splashes.

⇦ In the steam spring area to the east of Námafjall in the Mývatn District (Mývatnssveit) there is a large number of mud pots (solfataras), where the blue mud boils and simmers, sending up air bubbles in the thick mud which, when bursting, form concentric circles on the surface of the mud pot.

⇧
A complete contrast to the mud pots is this clear-blue hot spring near Geysir in Haukadalur. The water is so clear that its surface is barely discernible. Down in the spring the walls are covered with sinter.

hot springs

Most famous of the Icelandic spouting hot springs is the Geysir in Haukadalur, which has given its name to all similar hot springs in the world. Geysir spouts very seldom now, but near by there are several boiling hot water springs, some of which erupt regularly, e.g. Strokkur (see picture on p. 112). The bowl of Geysir is 18 m wide and 1.3 m deep, and it is situated in the top of a low mound, built up of layers of siliceous sinter from the spring water. From the bottom of the bowl there is a vertical tube which is about 20 m deep and 3 m wide at the top, but it narrows as it goes down. It is believed that Geysir and Strokkur were both formed in a great earthquake in 1294. We are told in the Oddaverja

⇦ Strokkur ('Churn') is the name of this erupter which is close to Geysir in Haukadalur. They are both believed to be situated in the same fissure, Strokkur being much smaller, however. It lets off abrupt and short spouts, which occur fairly regularly. Geysir, on the other hand, is reluctant to give spectacular performances any more and erupts only very rarely now.

A spectacular hot spring area is to be found at Hveravellir on Kjölur near the Langjökull glacier. Most of the hot springs are rather small. Some are calm and clear-blue ponds, while others eject boiling water and steam. Many of the hot springs have created real works of art out of the sinter that accumulates around their openings.

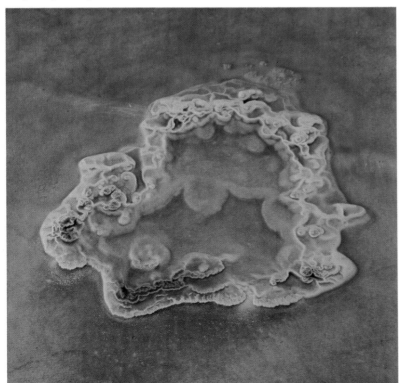

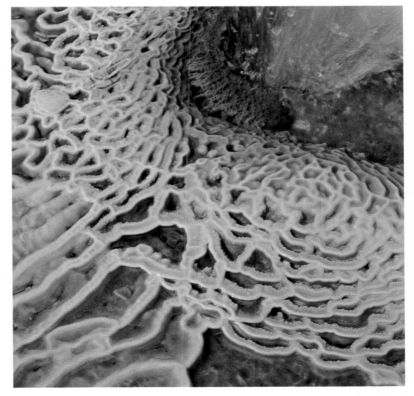

At Hveravellir layers of sinter have piled up to form large domes around the hot springs. Near the top of the main dome there is a calm and clear-blue hot spring in a good-sized bowl, while further up there is one called 'Roaring Mound' or 'Roaring Geyser', a cinter cone with two openings.

Annal that '...at Haukadalur two big hot water springs came into existence, whereas others which had been there before disappeared'. Research based on the time needed to build up the siliceous sinter mound, and dated volcanic ash layers in the soil below it supports this dating. After 1800 Geysir is often mentioned in foreign books on travel in Iceland, but around 1900 Geysir eruptions decreased in number, and in 1916 they stopped completely. In 1935 the eruptions started again after the water level in the bowl had been lowered, reducing the cooling of the water surface in the bowl. The Geysir eruptions were then and later studied by Dr. Trausti Einarsson, who explains them as follows: 'Into the vertical channel of Geysir the water enters at a temperature of 125 °C. through smaller passages coming from greater depths. At the bottom of the main tube the boiling point is about 132 °C. when the water is standing high in the bowl, and therefore the water does not boil at the bottom. At a depth of 10 m in the pipe the boiling point is about 120 °C., and there the temperature sometimes reaches that level and even higher, and boiling of the water there generates an eruption'.

It is not sufficient, however, for the water to reach a boiling point to start an eruption. The water has to be overheated by 4–5 °C. above the boiling point. The boiling then generates a sudden explosion, and the water above is thrown into the air. The explosive boiling produces the well-known rumbling noise just before the starting of an eruption, which is really the result of a long chain of explosions in the water. In powerful Geysir eruptions the water column can reach a height of 40–60 m, and it may continue for about 10 minutes. Towards the end a steam column emerges from the nearly empty tube.

Strokkur is of a similar type and is situated on the same fissure as Geysir, but it is much smaller. The highest temperature recorded in Iceland is 280 °C at a depth of about 1200 m in a drill-hole at Námaskarð, but the deepest hole drilled so far is in Reykjavík, 2200 m deep with a temperature of 146 °C.

This is a view into one of the openings of 'Roaring Geyser' at Hveravellir. Apparently it is not considered particularly silent when it periodically emits a big jet of steam.

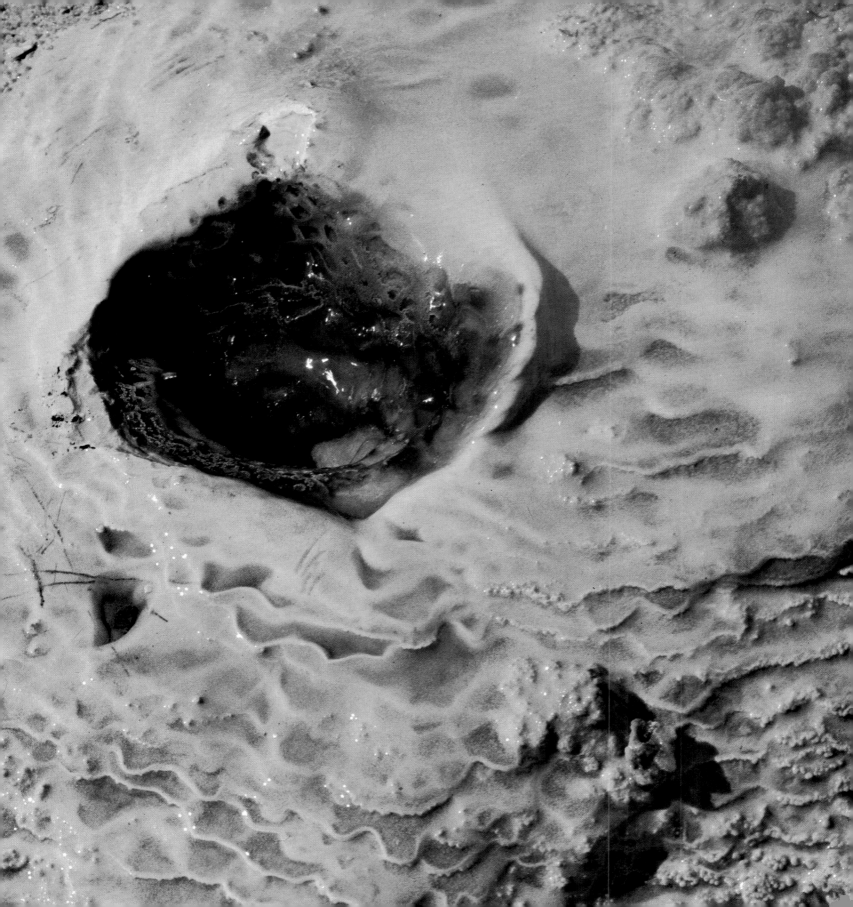

volcanoes

There is often a considerable relationship between volcanic and hot spring activity. Sometimes new hot springs are forerunners of volcanic eruptions, and often hot spring areas develop on the spot after the cessation of the volcanic activity. It is a volcanic eruption when hot materials break through the earth crust or when gases explode underneath the surface, resulting in the formation of an explosive crater, even if no lava or tephra comes to the surface. Spouting hot springs are not classified as volcanic eruptions in spite of the relationship between the two.

In and under the earth's crust is magma, at least in volcanic areas. The term magma applies to the molten rock still within the earth. That it is molten is naturally a guess because no one has ever seen magma proper, only the volcanic material that comes to the surface of the earth

Hekla is Iceland's most famous volcano. To the left is a view from the summit of Hekla over the top crater, which last erupted in 1947, towards the lava of 1913, Laufafell and Rauðfossafjöll. Below is a side view of Hekla as seen from Þjórsárdalur.

during eruptions, but such a material may have changed due to its contact with the upper rock-layers of the crust and reduced pressure. Geologically Iceland is a young country, almost completely built up by volcanic rocks. The basalt formation, which forms the oldest part of the country, was built up of lava layers one on top of the other to a pile of some kilometres in Tertiary times. During the subsequent ice ages the eruptions continued under the ice sheet and then the tuff mountains were built up. In discussions of volcanoes in Iceland, this term usually only applies to volcanic areas where eruptions have taken place since the last ice-age, which is considered to have ended about 10 000 years ago. These post-glacial volcanic areas are mainly in a broad belt lying over the middle of the country from south-west to north-east, split into two parts at the southern end as shown on the map on page 157, but outside this belt are the areas of Snæfellsnes and Öræfajökull. The direction of the volcanic fissures in the southern part of this

The Lakagígar craters number 100–115, all of them in a row of fissure in the SW-NE direction, which came into being in 1783. The whole fissure is about 25 km long. The tuff mountain Laki, which is situated near the centre of the fissure, burst open on both sides far up into the slopes during the eruption. Above is a view from Laki along the crater row to the south-west, but below is a view from a 90 m high red cinder cone, situated 3.5 km to the south-west, along the crater row to Laki.

area is mainly from south-west to north-east, but north of Vatnajökull the prevailing direction of the fissures is S to N.

It is reasonable to ask how many volcanoes there are in Iceland and how many of them are active. This question, however, is not an easy one to answer. In this connection it should be kept in mind that not all volcanoes are mountains. A volcano may be a fissure or a depression. Many explosive craters are examples of the latter. Several volcanic cones or a row of craters may develop along one fissure. If they have all been erupting at the same time, it is reasonable to call them all just one volcano. But if a new fissure opens up a century or so later, either as a continuation of the former or parallel to it near by, it is debatable whether the new fissure is a separate volcano or not. Another difficulty arises when a new lava flow completely inundates old craters. Furthermore, volcanoes under glaciers are common in Iceland and they are very difficult to count. Based on the period since the last ice age, the number of volcanoes in Iceland has been estimated to be definitely above 150 and most likely more than 200. But how many of these volcanoes are active, i.e. how many of them have erupted in historical time, which in Iceland covers the last

Ljótipollur ('Ugly Pool'), near Landmannalaugar, is one of the most beautiful explosive craters in Iceland. In form it is reminiscent of both calderas and explosive fissures. In explosive eruptions the volcanic material consists almost exclusively of cinders (tephra), and there is very little or no lava.

11 centuries, indicating that they might erupt again? The number of active volcanoes in Iceland has on this basis been estimated to be about 30. The total number of eruptions in Iceland since the settlement is nearly 200 because during the last few centuries there has been a volcanic eruption every 5th or 6th year on the average. Thus, Iceland is one of the most active volcanic areas on earth, but it is not least the variety of the Icelandic volcanoes which makes them interesting to volcanologists for field study. Almost all existing types of volcanoes can be found here and some of them are very rare outside Iceland.

Volcanoes formed by the opening of a fissure usually erupt only once. The most famous volcano in Iceland, Mt. Hekla, does not, however, follow this rule as this firy mountain ridge has been built up in several eruptions out of a fissure that has the usual SW-NE direction prevailing in this area. When the eruption started on the 29th March 1947, the Hekla cracked open along the whole mountain ridge, which has this direction, and the lava flowed down the slopes on both sides. The Hekla does not only present a prominent view from the lowland to the south, but also from the highlands and from the sea. Viewed in the direction of the fissure, its main contours are like those of a cone (stratovolcano), but a side-view from the Þjórsárdalur valley makes it look like a characteristic volcanic ridge. The length of the Hekla is about 10 km, and the fissure which opens up when the mountain itself erupts is about 5 km long. Since the eruption of 1947 the highest peak of Hekla has been 1491 m (see picture on p.116). Hekla's eruptions are mixed, i.e. it erupts both tephra and lava. Its history of eruptions over a period of about 7000 years can be studied with fair reliability. The mountain itself has been built up almost entirely in post-glacial time, but it rests on a foundation of mainly palagonite tuffs and breccias (Móberg) from the ice-age. The Hekla was a mountain at the time of the settlement as its oldest name indicates (Heklufell, 'Mount Hekla'). The Hekla erupted several times before

the settlement as many eruptions must have been needed to built up such a mountain. This is also indicated by numerous prehistoric tephra layers. But a long time had elapsed since the last eruption and the lava fields were covered with vegetation at the time of the settlement. Otherwise the settlers would not have built their farms in the lava areas near Hekla. The first written sources about an eruption in Hekla are to be found in the annals of 1104, which has the following entry: 'The first eruption of fire in Heklufell'. This means no doubt that this was the first eruption of Hekla after the settlement, and now it is considered quite certain that the Þjórsárdalur valley was devastated and abandoned as early as this eruption. It is likely that no less than 2–3 centuries had passed then since the last eruption of Hekla, except possibly for small eruptions which had not attracted much attention, if they happened after the settlement at all. Never since has such a long time elapsed between Hekla eruptions. The next eruptions occurred in 1158, 1206, and 1222. In 1300 an eruption started about 11th July and lasted for 12 months with big earthquakes, tephra-fall, famine and the death of people. The references of the annals to these eruptions are brief but to the point: A 1341 entry: 'Fire in Heklufell with a hard year and tephra-fall; many areas were abandoned. Darkness as great by day as by a winter night' (A. regii). – '…sheep and cattle died in Rangárvellir, and nearly five

⇨
Two-drive vehicles can be driven across lava and tephra plains by the side of Lakagígar. Great care should be taken not to cause damage to this unique phenomenon of nature by driving vehicles up the fragile crater rims. The only way to explore the craters is to walk.

Lakagígar are now moss-covered in many places and in the hollows the moss gives way like a thick carpet. Craters and lava, however, are dominant landscape features here with red lava rocks and black cinders contributing to the profusion of colours. This picture was taken from the crater row just to the south-west of Laki. Here the fissure, which came into being in the 'Skaftá Fires' of 1783, continues its course up the mountain. The crater row reaches as high as the middle of the mountain side.

This is the only one of the Lakagígar craters which extends below the ground-water level. There is a clear-blue pond in the bottom of it, surrounded by precipitous walls, covered with reddish lava splashes. In between the lava formations the soft greyish-green moss is ubiquitous. From this crater enormous lava channels lie in southerly and easterly directions. Although they are now beautifully adorned with variegated vegetation, it is still easy to see what enormous quantities of lava were produced by this crater in 1783.

121

◁ The lava from the Lakagígar of the 'Skaftá Fires' of 1783 covers an area of 565 km². It flowed down the river-beds of the Skaftá and the Hverfisfljót, radically changing their courses. Further down the lava swallowed up anything that happened to be in its path, including pastures, homefields, grassland and human habitation. This is how the more westerly lava stream looks today. It is covered with a thick layer of moss, although it still clearly reveals traces of the cataclysmic upheaval which caused the lava to surge forward in this place almost two centuries ago.

△
Dimmuborgir to the east of Mývatn is an area of most peculiar lava formations which owe their origin to a volcanic activity of great magnitude. There a number of bushes grow between lava rocks of varying shapes with holes, hollows and openings. There are paths throughout this sanctuary, but many a visitor has lost his way in this labirynth of shattered lava formations, making his stay here a little longer than originally planned.

123

From Dyngjufjöll above Drekagil there is a beautiful view to Herðu- ⇨
breið. The dark stripes in the flat area show the main lava streams from
the Askja eruption of 1961, when lava flowed from new craters near
Öskjuop. Herðubreið is a table mountain. The volcanic eruptions
which built up the table mountains are considered to have occurred
under the ice-age glacier. The fires first melted a dome in the ice and
then a hole up through it. The basalt magma which emerged under-
went very sudden cooling in the melt-water, forming pillow lava and
tephra which later turned into palagonite tuff. The enveloping glacier
prevented the spread of the tephra with the result that the mountain
grew higher and higher until it emerged from the surface of the water
which had filled the opening in the glacier. In this way the mountain
formed an insulating collar around the vent which enabled the volcanic
activity to change from an explosive eruption to an effusive one with
the production of lava which accumulated on top of the tuff socle.

⚐
Helgafell of the Vestmannaeyjar is one of the most beautiful volcanic
cones in Iceland. In fact it is considered an intermediary between two
volcanic types, a cone and an 'eldborg' ('rock castle'). It is known to
have erupted twice. In the former eruption an eldborg was built up in
an effusive eruption, producing considerable lava, but the latter was a
mixed eruption, giving birth to the cone which adorns Heimaey today. This latter eruption, however, occurred thousands of years before
Iceland was settled and therefore Helgafell is not considered an active
volcano. The picture shows Helgafell from the sea across Eiðið.
Heimaklettur is to the left and Klifið to the right.

districts were ruined'. A 1389–90 entry: 'A fire started ni Heklufell with such great force that the crash and a rumbling noise could be heard all over the country. Two farms, Skarð and Tjaldstaðir, were obliterated'. (Lögm. A.). The lava flow most likely engulfed both these farmsteads during this eruption. The next Hekla eruptions occurred in 1510, 1597, and 1636. One of the most violent eruptions of Hekla began on 13th February 1693. The tephra-fall was enormous, covering about 22,000 km² of land and about 55 farms in neighbouring districts were ruined or badly damaged. The longest eruption of Hekla in historical times began on the 5th April 1766 and lasted until April 1768. The initial phase was violent with a very heavy tephra-fall, and later up to 18 columns of fire could be seen coming out of the mountain at the same time. After this big eruption Hekla took a rest for 77 years, but the next eruption started on 2nd September 1845. Very detailed information is available on this eruption. There was a considerable tephra-fall, and often there was a total darkness in the middle of the day in neighbouring districts. The eruption column could be seen from Reykjavik, and its height was measured to be 4370 m above the peak of Hekla. There was also a considerable lava-flow from the eruption, covering 25 km² of land, and on the 23rd September the farmstead Næfurholt was abandoned when the lava-flow came close to it through the ravine of a brook near by, inun-

Above is a view from Herðubreiðarlindir over to Herðubreið. The table mountain form is quite clear, a belt of lava rocks at the top with palagonite tuff underneath (see legend to picture on p. 124). The pictures below were taken at the craters which came into being in the Askja eruption of 1961. It is a view in the direction of Herðubreið over the lava which flowed from Öskjuop and covered the old road to Askja. The craters still emit some smoke many years after the eruption.

Lava channels are quite common in Iceland. They occur in places where the lava originally flowed fast downhill along a kind of gully. Owing to the speed of the flow, little solidification takes place on the way. If the lava flow suddenly ceases at its source, the gully is emptied and these lava channels receive their present form. This is a picture of a newly-formed lava channel on Surtsey.

127

dating an area of cultivated grass land. The farm was moved after this eruption (see map on p. 162). There have also been several eruptions in the neighbourhood of Hekla, including one in 1878 and another in 1913. As mentioned above, an eruption in Hekla itself started on 29th March 1947, and it continued for nearly 13 months. The eruption which started in, and close to, Hekla on 5th May 1970 is described in a separate chapter (see p. 162–167).

More than half of the active volcanoes in Iceland are of the crater-row type, i.e. craters formed along a fissure, 35 km to 100 m long or even less. The craters on the same fissure may produce both tephra and lava. Lakagígar, for example, are such a mixed crater-row. – The Lakagígar were formed in an eruption which began on Whit-Sunday, June 8th 1783, and lasted until the beginning of February the following year. It is by far the biggest lava eruption on earth in historical times and possibly the biggest one after the ice age. There is hardly any doubt that Lakagígar are one of the most impressive crater-rows that have been built up by a single fissure eruption. The detailed contemporary description of this eruption by the Reverend Jón Stein-grímsson (the 'Fire Manuscript') is a reliable eye-witness account of the course of events of the Lakagígar eruption. The fissure which opened up during the eruption is about 25 km long. It almost cuts through the 'móberg' (palago-nite tuffs and breccias) mountain Laki, which is situated about the middle of the fissure. From the beginning on June 8th until the 29th July 1783 only the crater-row south-west of Laki was active and the lava flowed down the river-bed of the Skaftá, filling its canyon with lava masses. On the 29th of July the fissure north-east of Laki opened up and thereupon most of the lava flow followed the river-bed of Hverfisfljót. The 1783 lava flow engulfed 2 churches and 13 farmsteads, and 30 other farms were badly damaged. The stunting of grass growth all over Iceland during the summer of 1783 was, however, far more disastrous. The main reason for the ruining of grass growth was the bluish haze caused by the enormous amount of volcanic gases released from the lava. This bluish haze lay all over the country and was even noticed in other European countries. Most likely it was mainly SO_2 gases which stunted the growth of grass. By comparison with the SO_2 gas percentage measured in the basaltic Surtsey magma it has been estimated that about 10 million tons of SO_2 gases were released during the Laki eruption. The stunting of the grass and possibly also its fluor contamination from the tephra-fall caused a catastrophic starvation of livestock. During this worst famine in the history of Iceland the population was reduced by nearly 24%. The main cause was the Lakagígar eruption, but the winter of 1783/84 was also very severe, ice and fire thus joining their destructive forces. No wonder that this was called the Haze Famine. The lava-flow from Lakagígar covers 565 km² of land, and its estimated volume is 12 km³. The Lakagígar is one of the most remarkable natural phenomena in Iceland. The craters are different in size and form, a mixture of explosive craters and lava-craters. Sometimes there are smaller craters on the slopes of bigger ones. They are, therefore, difficult to count, but their number is around 100. The colours of the Lakagígar area are spectacular. There are black ash cones, red-burned scoria and lava, and moss-covered craters and lava streams. It must be kept in mind, however, that this highland vegetation is very sensitive, and all nature lovers are very anxious to keep this virgin land of natural wonders unspoiled so that coming generations may also enjoy its beauty and marvel at the formidable power hidden underneath. Explosive craters are common in Iceland, the youngest of them being the Víti in the Askja volcano, which was formed in an explosive eruption on 29th March 1875. Askja has erupted several times, last time in the autumn of 1961, when after more than 30 years of rest new hot springs broke through the surface, followed by a volcanic eruption which started on October 26th 1961 and continued until the beginning of 1962.

⇨

On a map of Iceland made by Bishop Guðbrandur Þorláksson before 1585 Hekla is shown to be violently active and it contains the following comment: 'Hekla perpetuis damnata estib. et nivib. horrendo boatu lapides evomit', i.e. 'Hekla, which is cursed with eternal fires and snow, ejects rocks, making horrible noise'. The isolation of Iceland in the Middle Ages and the vague news of Hekla eruptions reaching other European countries gave rise to the rumour that the entrance to Hell was to be found in Iceland and that black damned souls could be seen hovering over Hekla.

finguitur limes inter vi a u_y uwetchm

N DLEN
G A FIOR
G.

Hekla *perpetuis
damnata æstib. et ni-
uib. horrendo boatu
lapides evomit*

Fiske=
notn.

Skabt a.

Mydals Iokul.

Oddi.

Eyafialla
Iokul.

Solheima
Iokul.

Breida holt
stadar

rum
hic
as, vt

Meda.

island born in fire

A submarine eruption is in many ways similar to an eruption occurring underneath a glacier when melt-water is dammed up by the surrounding ice-sheet. When a volcanic fissure opens up on the sea-bed and the molten lava streams out, the cooling is so rapid that all the volcanic material immediately changes into scoria or tephra, building up a cone from the sea bed, or is thrown up in the air and scattered over the surrounding area. Light tephra ash floats on the sea, but the gases from the magma are mixed with the steam column that rises from the boiling sea to considerable heights above the submarine volcano.

This is how the birth of a new island in the sea began in an area where there had been a 130 m depth of water about 33 km from the Landeyjarsandur coastline and about 5.5 km. WSW of Geirfuglasker, the nearest skerry of the Vestmannaeyjar islands, the southernmost spot of Iceland until then. Eye-witness accounts of the birth of islands are

very rare, but we have some in the case of Surtsey, which was the name given to the new island later. The fishing vessel Isleifur II of the Vestmannaeyjar was fishing 4 miles west of Geirfuglasker the night before the 14th November 1963. At 6.30 in the morning the crew had finished to pay out the long line and went down to their quarters to have a cup of morning coffee. When they about 7 o'clock in the morning came up on deck again, they noticed a smell of sulphur, for which they could not find any reason. Shortly afterwards the sea around the ship unexpectedly became unquiet, and at daybreak within the next hour, they noticed an obscure mass rising out of the sea south-east of the vessel. They soon realized that black smoke clouds were rising out of the sea. This could only be a submarine eruption, and the skipper called the Vestmannaeyjar radio station, reported his observations and sailed his ship nearer to the scene for a closer study. Half a mile away the sea was

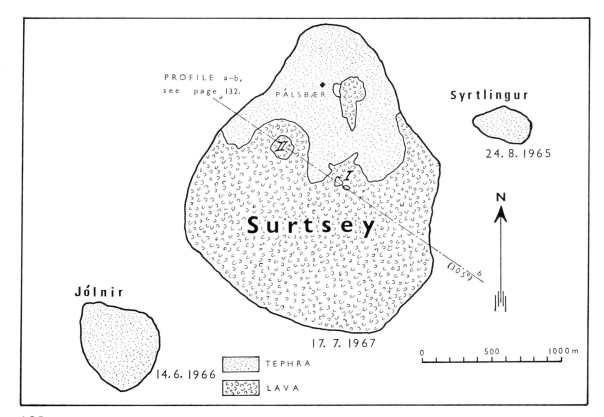

PROFILE a–b, see page 132.

PÁLSBÆR

Syrtlingur

24. 8. 1965

N

Surtsey

(305°)

Jólnir

17. 7. 1967

14. 6. 1966

TEPHRA

LAVA

0   500   1000 m

The map shows the size of Surtsey on July 17th 1967 and the islets of Syrtlingur and Jólnir on August 24th 1965 and June 14th 1966 respectively. Today there are only shallows where Syrtlingur and Jólnir used to be.

An eruption began in the sea in the morning of 14th November 1963 just over 33 km off the Landeyjarsandur and only 23 km away from the town of Vestmannaeyjar. This is an aerial view, taken at 10.30 a.m. on 16th November 1963. The height of the eruption column was then up to 9 km.

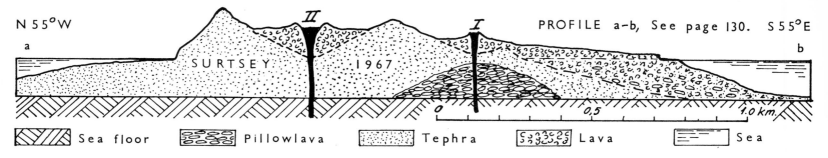

SURTSEY 1967

Sea floor   Pillowlava   Tephra   Lava   Sea

A profile of Surtsey in 1967 after both Surtur II and Surtur I had erupted lava. This profile, a–b on the map on p. 130, is intended to cut through both of these vents and therefore lies approximately in the direction N 55°W to S 55°E. Probably there is a socle of pillow lava around the Surtur I vent a good distance towards the surface of the sea. Then tephra accumulated on top of it, forming an island in the sea. The vent of Surtur II, on the other hand, was formed through the tephra layers that came from Surtur I, which at that time was close to reaching the surface of the sea. Therefore, there is probably no or very little pillow lava under Surtur II. A lava-producing effusive eruption began when the sea no longer found its way to the magma in the vent. Where lava flowed to the sea, layers of mixed tephra and lava were formed on the sea-bed, some of it, perhaps, appearing as pillow lava. Tephra or cinders is the raw material for palagonite tuff.

A view of Surtsey just after it emerged from the sea at 10.30 a.m. on November 16th 1963. Aircraft were constantly encircling the eruption column. The Vestmannaeyjar and the south coast of Iceland are in the background.

getting so rough that it was not felt safe to go any closer, and by that time they were quite sure of what was happening. Watching this new submarine eruption for some time, it seemed to them that the activity was increasing and the fissure evidently lengthened during the time they stayed there. The news of a volcanic activity in the sea soon spread and the first aircraft were encircling above the place at 10.30 a.m. Then the eruption was still gathering momentum. Stones were flying out of the black tephra column, which then had reached a height of 100 to 150 m. At the same time the eruption column grew steadily higher, and at 11 a.m. it had reached a height of about 4 km. The length of the fissure had then increased to about 400 m, erupting at four places simultaneously. Expectedly, the direction of the fissure was near to the usual N35°E to S35°W for the southern part of the country. Concentric waves could be seen coming from the volcanic area, and the sea nearest to the fissure had a peculiar brownish-green colour. Dark patches of floating tephra were drifting about and carried away by the wind. In the evening of that same day the coastguard vessel Albert came to the eruption area and determined its position. Then the waves started to break on shallows, and it was clearly not long until the fire-ridge would break through the surface of the sea. The following night a new island was born. This new submarine eruption showed only few precursory signs of what was going to happen so it was really quite unexpected. Although seismographs in Reykjavik had shown weak trem-

⇨

This is the crater-bowl of Surtur II, from which lava flowed intermittently from April 4th 1964 to May 17th 1965. The crater-bowl, however, varied a great deal in size and shape. Sometimes the lava overflowed the crater rims and at other times it flowed through underground channels for considerable distances. Lethal gases hover over the crater. These are volatile substances released by the magma when it comes to the surface. One of the main substances in this blue haze, through which the sun barely penetrates, is sulphur dioxide in addition to water vapour. In the crater the lava boils and bubbles at a temperature of 1150°–1200°C.

ors the week before the eruption was first noticed, it was not possible with any certainty to determine their place of origin. In Vestmannaeyjar and at Vík í Mýrdal on the coast of the mainland some sulphur smell was noted a few days before the eruption was first seen. The night before the 13th November the trawler Þorsteinn Þorskabítur was engaged in fishery research to the south-west of Vestmannaeyjar when it was noticed that barely 4 km south-west of the place where the eruption started the temperature was 2.4° higher within a limited area than in the surrounding sea. It can now be said that the weak tremors, the sulphur smell and the increased temperature in the sea indicate that the submarine eruption had started some time before it was noticed, but that it most likely developed slowly in the beginning. It is probable, therefore, that warm vapour had been escaping from the volcanic area for some days before the crew of the fishing vessel Ísleifur II first witnessed the eruption.

Already the day after the eruption was first noticed, the island was 10 m above sea level and a great amount of volcanic material was added every day as the eruption was almost continuous. The eruption column frequently reached a height of 9 km and then often looked rather threatening to those who saw it from the Vestmannaeyjar, not least when the wind carried the ash from the column over the islands. During the first few days of the eruption the weather was favourable for following the growth of the island, both from the air and from sea. On the third day the height of the island was about 40 m, but it was split longitudinally. The sea, therefore, entered the vents between the explosions when they were not continuous. The enormous amount of volcanic material, which in only a few days had built up a mountain 170 m high measured from the sea floor, was very loose, mostly tephra, so that it was easily washed away and re-formed by the shifting action of ocean waves and the wind. The fire, however, was usually the strongest agent. The island continued to grow,

Above lava splashes fly out of one of the August vents of Surtur I. Below there is an aerial view of the area surrounding the crater-bowl of Surtur II, while no flowing lava can be seen on the surface.

◁

At night the Surtsey scene often resembled a fireworks display. During the night before August 16th 1964 the ocean breeze was cool, but the radiant heat from the crater Surtur II was comfortable. At short intervals there were explosions in the bubbling lava, causing red-hot splashes to fly high up in the air.

and on the 20th November it had reached a height of 70 m above sea level. Its length was then about 900 m and its width nearly 700 m. When the wind direction changed, the sea was blocked from reaching the vents on the lee-side, but soon the ocean waves broke into the vents from another side. Thus the demolishing forces of the ocean fought a great battle with the creative forces of the volcanic eruption which were engaged in building up a new island, and in this struggle there were gains and losses on both sides. The craters on the island soon decreased in number, only one or two of them usually being active at a time. In general it can be said that there were explosive eruptions at irregular intervals when the sea was able to enter the craters, but as soon as a reef was formed that was big enough to keep the sea out, a continuous eruption started. It was much more productive in building up the island as enormous amounts of tephra were then permanently ejected out of the crater, strengthening the crater walls. The flying bombs could then reach a height of about 2500 m. This eruption was not followed by any big noise. There was only a heavy roar when the eruption was most powerful and the bombs were falling on the sides of the crater or into the sea where they exploded. Thus the eruption continued to transport new material from the bowels of the earth up to the surface. The vents shifted from one place to another, the old took a rest and new ones came into being. The island was officially baptized Surtsey after the giant Surtur of the old Eddaic poem Völuspá. At the end of March 1964 Surtsey was more than one km^2 in area, about 1100 m in width and 1400 m in length. Although the island thus had reached a considerable size, it was by no means thought it would be permanent because the winter storms had shown themselves to be most destructive, even compared with the enormous power of the fire. The only hope for the survival of Surtsey was the possibility of sufficient tephra material stopping seawater from entering the vent, preventing its contact with the molten magma masses. This happened on

◁
Three lava vents appeared in a fissure that opened in Old Surtur (Surtur I) on August 19th 1966, a crater which had not been active for 2¹/₂ years. The craters, which produced large amounts of lava, were called 'The August Vents'. The picture was taken in the evening of August 27th 1966. Then lava flowed from two of the crater-cones. The volcanic island of Jólnir, which was first seen on December 26th 1965, is in the background. Volcanic activity ceased there altogether about the middle of August 1966, and in the October of that same year Jólnir disappeared in the sea again.

The first trips to Surtsey were made by sea. The conditions varied a great deal so that many of the early explorers got soaking wet when they landed on the island. Rubber dinghies were by far the most suitable means of transportation between the ships and the island. Some of them were propelled by oars, while others were fitted with an outboard motor. Special skill was required for landing on the island when the sea was rough, and similarly great care was needed on departure from the island. For a while the sandy beach of Surtsey could be used as a landing-strip for small aircraft after the bigger stones had been removed. Take-off was often rather difficult when the sand was too soft, limiting the number of passengers the aircraft could take. For a time Syrtlingur ruined all possibilities of landing on the island by its hot ash eruption. A helicopter was also used a few times for transportation between the vessels and the island or between the Vestmannaeyjar Airport and Surtsey, and this was the easiest way of travelling.

At the end of May 1965 a volcanic activity began in the sea about 600 m ENE of Surtsey, giving birth to the island of Syrtlingur, which reached a height of 70 m and a length of 650 m. The above picture is of the hot ash eruption of Syrtlingur on July 3rd 1965 as it was seen from Surtsey. Below is an aerial view of the volcanic island of Jólnir, taken on May 24th 1966.

April 4th 1964, and from that date onwards the Surtsey eruption was very similar to one on land. Then the wall between the crater and the sea had become very thick, and an effusive eruption started by the crater being filled with red-hot magma from which glowing lava streams began to head for the sea. The intensity of the lava eruption fluctuated considerably, however. Sometimes the magma level in the crater subsided, but in between it overflowed the crater rims to such an extent that red-hot lava streams flowed down the tephra slopes which were now gradually being covered with thin layers of lava. The result was a big lava dome which by the end of April had reached a height of 90 m, the lava flow being very extensive at this time with many lava streams heading for the sea simultaneously. Where the lava met the sea huge columns of steam rose high in the air. In places the lava was seen to flow red-hot along the sea-bed as if it were insulated from the water by enveloping steam. Therefore, the temperature of the sea rose substantially in these places. At other times the lava hardened very suddenly, turning to scoria as soon as it came in contact with the sea. The sea-surge ground this material to glassy sand which now constitutes the beaches of Surtsey. At the end of April the surface flow of lava discontinued for a few months although the lava in the crater was constantly red-hot and bubbling. During this period some lava apparently flowed through underground channels to the sea, strengthening the base of Surtsey. As soon as there was a pause in the lava flow to the sea, the sea-surge began to break down the edge of the lava. It was really quite surprising how soon sea-cliffs were formed and big rocks lying on the beach turned into boulders rounded by the sea. All these rocks, however, helped to ward off the attacks of the sea. When the lava resumed its flow from the crater on July 9th 1964, it made its way over the old lava and fell off sea-cliffs formed by the sea-surge, but some of it travelled through underground channels and emerged through holes in the lower parts of the lava dome or down

⇨

Syrtlingur was continuously active on most of July 3rd 1965 while material for the foundations of Pálsbær, the hut of the Surtsey Research Society, was being taken ashore. The first foundations were set down in the Surtsey lava right opposite Syrtlingur, which then buried them in a thick layer of ashes so that a new site had to be selected near the lagoon where Pálsbær is situated now.

⇧
Jólnir was violently active on May 24th 1966 when this picture was taken from a ship. When the sea gets into direct contact with the magma, the latter disintegrates with the result that cinders fly up in the air. This is the so-called hot ash eruption.

140

⇨
When a vent emits lava which turns into hard rock through slow solidification it is called an effusive eruption. A brook of water digs a channel in the ground with banks of varying height. A stream of lava, on the other hand, often builds up a ridge underneath its course with lava flowing off on both sides as can be seen in the picture to the right.

The first landing on Jólnir took place on May 20th 1966. These pictures show the second landing there on May 24th. Below is the rubber dinghy used for the landing with Surtsey in the background. The picture above was taken at the foot of the crater cone on the southern end of the island. Drizzling rain mixed with the tephra-fall from the eruption. Volcanic bombs had fallen in many places. Many of them were the size of a man's fist, whereas some were as big as 80 cm in diameter.

by the oldest sea-cliffs. Although the lava flow from the crater evidently varied a great deal, the amount of the flow during the first few months of the effusive eruption was very substantial, and it has been estimated that the bulk of volcanic solids produced was about the same in the explosive eruption as in the lava eruption up to the end of 1964. On the 15th December of that year the area of Surtsey was 213 hectares, 123 hectares of which were covered by lava. The lava flow discontinued for a while on May 17th 1965, but about that time steam was seen to come out of the sea about 600 m ENE of Surtsey and by the end of May there were clear signs of a volcanic activity there with a new island being in creation. This new island had reached a height of 16 m and a diameter of 170 m by June 8th. Four days later this island had gone, but it reappeared on June 14th. Two days later the island had reached a height of 37 m and a length of 190 m and the name that was given to it was Syrtlingur ('Little Surtur'). On September 17th Syrtlingur reached its maximum height of 70 m, its length then being 650 m. After this date the Syrtlingur eruption became less and less active, whereas the demolishing action of the sea gained the upper hand with the result that it was seen for the last time on October 17th 1965. On December 26th 1965 a volcanic activity was noticed about 900 m south-west of Surtsey, and on January 2nd a new island emerged there with two active vents. It disappeared, however, within a few days. Thus, this new island emerged and submerged again and again until April 7th, when it disappeared for the 5th time, but once again it reappeared on April 14th, and on May 12th it had again grown to a length of 560 m and a height of 40 m. The eruption column was more than 6000 m high on May 20th, when the first landing on this island took place. About this time it received the name Jólnir because it had first been seen on Boxing Day. Jólnir was visited again on May 24th (see pictures on p.142) when the visitors reached the foot of the crater cone that had developed on the southern part of the island. At the

⇨

Often the Surtsey lava flowed long distances underground and sometimes it did not emerge to the surface until it had reached as far as the sea-shore. Yet openings were sometimes found in the roof of the channel, through which the rapid stream of the red-hot lava could be studied. The temperature of the lava in these underground channels was apparently similar to that of the lava in the crater, i.e. 1150–1160°C. Therefore, the heat radiating from it was enormous.

No flowing surface lava could be seen near the vents of Old Surtur (Surtur I) on 19th May 1967, but then lava flowed along underground channels to openings near the sea-shore where jets of steam could be seen rising in the air. The vents were very hot, and it was very hard to climb the crater cones because of noxious gases from the magma.

In this picture, taken on 29th August 1966, a lava-fall is seen to flow off older sea-cliffs formed by the sea-surge after the first lava flow on Surtsey. The lava stream transports solidified lava junks just as ordinary rivers bring down ice floes.

A lava stream issuing from the crater in the background down over older lava on August 29th 1966. The lava stream often changes its course as the lava piles up, filling older fissures and hollows.

Sometimes the precipitations on Surtsey were colourful beyond description: They were orange, yellow green, red, yellow orange and sometimes bluish. The lava assumed these colours because of the condensation of gases which escaped from holes and cracks in the lava.

Precipitations in the lava below Old Surtur (Surtur I) were most colourful. From a distance the lava often looked as if it were covered with moss. The yellow green colour is due to sodium and potassium sulphates, but other sulphates and pure sulphur also led to precipitations.

148

Here new lava inundates older lava-flows which have already been coloured by precipitations. The new lava advances inside a semi-hardened crust as if it rolled forward in a bag. Constantly, however, red-hot embers can be seen in the lava, and sometimes the crust bursts, releasing a thinner material until that, too, has developed an enveloping crust.

149

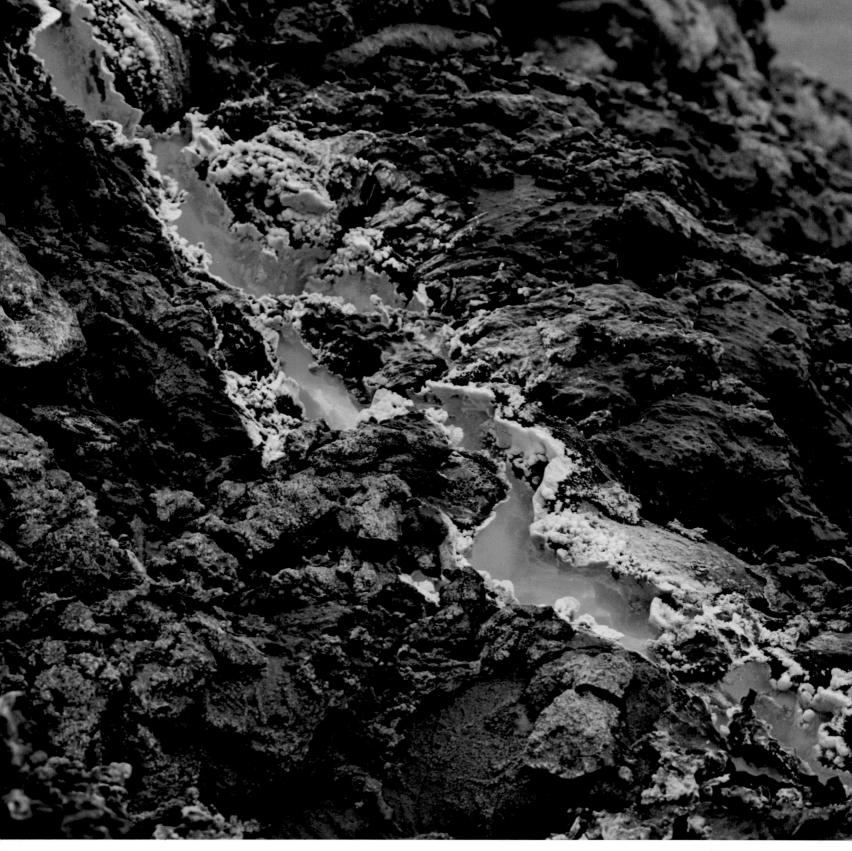

beginning of August the Jólnir eruption began to decline very sharply and ceased altogether by the middle of the month. But the sea-surge continued its activity and in October it disappeared for good after an intermittent existence for 10 months. Its maximum size had been an area of 28 hectares and a height of 70 m.

Let us now revert to Surtsey. In the morning of 19th August 1966 a fissure opened in the crater called Old Surtur (marked I on the map on p. 130), which had then been dormant for 2½ years, i.e. since the end of January 1964. This fissure was about 220 m long and 7–15 m wide, emitting a 100 m wide lava stream which headed for the sea. Subsequently three lava cones developed on this fissure, two of which adjoined, whereas the third one was situated at some distance from the others. These vents were called 'the August Vents', and they produced very large quantities of lava. On August 21st the lava flow was estimated to be 5–10 m³/sec at a short distance from the vent. During this period continuous tremors were felt on Surtsey, being particularly noticeable in the hut which had been erected (Pálsbær). The lava flow from the August Vent continued right until the end of 1966, bringing radical changes to the Surtsey landscape. For instance, the lava inundated a site on the eastern part of the island which had been chosen for the Surtsey hut before Syrtlingur began its activity 600 m off the shore, burying the site in a thick layer of ashes, which, however, had been washed away by the sea-surge when the site was engulfed by the lava from the August

To the left embers can be seen in a crack in the Surtsey lava, its edges being adorned with variegated precipitations. In the top right-hand picture scientists are at work, measuring the temperature of a lava stream. To the right is Pálsbær and the lagoon before and after the lava flow of January 1967, which halted its advance 120 m away from Pálsbær. Above an attempt is being made at pumping sea-water into a lava stream to change its course by cooling.

vents being most productive, however. Yet the lava flow was clearly on the wane, and much of it passed through underground channels down to the sea-shore. On June 5th 1967 flowing lava on Surtsey was seen for the last time. If we look upon that date as the last day of the Surtsey eruption it had lasted for three years and almost seven months being the second longest eruption in Iceland in historical time, only a few months shorter than the 'Myvatn Fires' of 1725–1729. These eruptions behaved similarly in many ways, even though one of them started on the sea-bed and the other in the highlands. When the Surtsey eruption ceased, the new island was 2.8 km² in area.

No Icelandic eruption has been studied more assiduously than the Surtsey one. This research still goes on even though no lava flows there any more. The history of the eruption has been meticulously recorded right from its beginning, and data collection was carried out on the island both during the eruption and after it ceased. This work will be continued for years to come because this island presents a unique opportunity for a study of the genesis of land right from its throes of birth as well as of its formative history, the chief agents of which are the sea-surge, rain the sun and the wind. Of particular interest are the biologi-

Vent. But on January 1st 1967 it was noticed that a fissure had opened up in the north side of the crater wall of Surtur I, from which lava flowed into the lagoon in front of Pálsbær (see pictures on p. 151). The next day the lava had more than half-filled the lagoon and there was some anxiety for the safety of Pálsbær. Such worries were needless, however, because at this time a fissure had opened on the inside of the crater wall. Already on January 3rd more lava was flowing from it than from the north side, where the lava flow stopped altogether on January 5th when the edge of the lava was at a distance of 120 m from Pálsbær. From the beginning of January until 5th June 1967 the lava flow from the August Vents in Surtur I was continuous, one of the

⇧

A number of lava streams were flowing parallel to the Surtsey sea-shore on January 7th 1967. Frequently a steam-cloud covered large areas of the shore.

⇨

The red-hot lava drops into the foaming sea-surge on the Surtsey shore. Every backward flow of the surf revealed the red-hot lava stream, whereas on its return all the scene disappeared in a steam-cloud.

cal aspects of these studies: How does life start on an island born of fire in the middle of the sea? These studies, however, have been made under difficult conditions. The point was aptly made by one of the geologists at work on the island when he commented to the effect that a big disadvantage of islands was their being surrounded by the sea. In the past geologists were certainly not used to having to practice seamanship along with their research work.

⇧

This surf is no different from that of any other ocean shore. But these cliffs and this sandy beach is only a few years old because this picture was taken on Surtsey on May 20th 1967 with a view towards the Vestmannaeyjar. The history of the development of Surtsey, which emerged from the sea from a depth of 130 m in one more or less continuous eruption, is very instructive for students of rare natural phenomena. No less interesting is the formative history of this new island. The sea with its breakers and currents, the rain and the wind are constantly busy transforming and moulding it. Their demolishing action is surprisingly effective. The best evidence of this is the speed with which the islands of Syrtlingur and Jólnir were swept away shortly after

the volcanic activity there ceased. Nobody dared to predict a permanent existence of Surtsey until an effusive eruption started, producing lava as a result of the slower cooling of the magma. Even the edge of the lava, which formed sloping lava flows down to the sea, has now been broken down by the surf and turned into precipitous sea-cliffs, skirted by a rock-strewn sandy beach. These rocks no longer resemble chunks of recent lava. Instead there are sea-worn boulders and gravel-banks between areas of finer sand. Many people would think the age of this land to be thousands of years, so much does the swift action of the forces of nature confuse our sense of time.

153

The colours of the precipitations on Surtsey presented a marvellous
spectacle, but they soon faded and completely disappeared in due
course. This is a view from Surtsey to the Vestmannaeyjar and the
mainland on January 9th 1967, with Mýrdalsjökull and Eyjafjallajökull
in the background. Lava is still flowing into the sea as can be seen by
the steam-cloud.

154

The Surtsey Society was founded for the purpose of organizing the co-operation of scientists and planning the whole body of Surtsey research. Originally only a committee was set up to assist Icelandic geologists in their Surtsey studies. Soon, however, great interest of overseas scientists in an active participation in these studies became manifest and the role of the Surtsey Society is an overall co-ordination and planning of all Surtsey research. The Society has already published four mimeographed works, 'Surtsey Research Progress Report I, II, III, and IV, and held two conferences in Reykjavik on the Surtsey research effort. The first conference was held in 1965, devoting almost all its time to biological studies, but the interest of biologists increased greatly after the lava flow began on April 4th 1964 because after that the survival of Surtsey was more or less secure. The latter conference was held in 1967, dealing with both biological and geological subjects in addition to many specialized branches of each. The Surtsey research effort is financially supported by the Icelandic government and Icelandic research funds, but in addition it has received generous grants from various overseas research funds as Surtsey is considered a unique field for some specialized research. In historical time only very few islands on earth have been known to be born of volcanic activity and become permanent geographical features. Up to now those few occasions have little or not at all given spur to scientific evolutionary research. Even when all life on the island of Krakatoa was eradicated in a volcanic eruption in 1883, hardly any research was done on the subsequent re-settlement of vegetation on the island. When the first biologist came to the island three years later, he found that 30 plants had already taken root there, and ten years later the whole island was covered by trees, including palm-trees, and other plants. A more detailed study was made of the Island of Ana-Krakatoa, but owing to much more favourable climatic conditions and the luxuriant vegetation on neighbouring islands it can hardly be compared with Surtsey, which is surrounded by the icy breakers of the North-Atlantic. The sea-surge washes its entire shore and its spray extends over the whole island. When the weather is rough, the wind churns up the salty tephra, and when Syrtlingur and Jólnir were in their prime, they covered Surtsey with ashes, stifling any bud which attempted settlement on the island. Owing to the biological research on Surtsey it has been made a sanctuary under the control of the Surtsey Research Society.

Evidently it will take a long time for vegetation to take root on the island. Nature is in no hurry. For the research effort this slow development is favourable, giving the researchers plenty of time to study every detail that might throw a new light on the origin of life in a sterile environment. Plant parts and seeds from neighbouring islands have been washed ashore and some beach plants have managed to take root in the upper parts of sandy beaches. Sea birds have already nested on Surtsey. In the upper part of the lava seedlings of moss have been found, probably brought from neighbouring islands by birds.

While ornitologists and botanists keep a watchful eye on any developments on land, oceanographers, marine biologists and algaologists are busy studying the sea around Surtsey, its submarine base and the sea-shore. Migratory birds that call at Surtsey on their way from more Southern lands have been studied to find out about the growth potential of seeds brought by them. An interesting subject for comparative study is vegetation on nunataks. Although the relationship between the two may not seem obvious, such glacier rocks are to some extent analogous to a volcanic island in the sea. To both, plants have to be carried a long way over barren and lifeless areas as far as vegetation is concerned. Therefore, the botanical research that has been carried out in recent years in Esjufjöll of the Vatnajökull glacier (see map on p. 48 and picture on p. 78) has been given considerable attention by those who are studying the formation of soil and vegetation on Surtsey, where samples of volcanic cinders are collected for the study of the development of their soil potential for plants.

An important geological aspect of the Surtsey research work has been detailed recording of the history of the eruption from its inception to its final phase to make the development of all its main factors accessible. The history of older eruptions in Iceland was recorded either by eye-witnesses or on the basis of second-hand accounts. Thus eyes and ears were the chief sources of information for the early annalists, some of their works giving a very clear account of the chain of events. Even today the eyes and ears of an observant spectator are very important research tools. Photographs of course, preserve the visual side of an eruption better than any human brain or even a detailed description. A photograph might even preserve an event that lasted only a fraction of a second, an event that might be unique and difficult to describe in words or explain satisfactorily. The recording of the history of an eruption, however, is not the only geological aspect of the research work. By measuring the quantity of the volcanic material produced within each period and by geochemical and geophysical research certain facts may be discovered which form a much more reliable basis for any general conclusions. Since the beginning of volcanic studies it has been clear that various gases are brought to the surface with the magma (see p. 117) and there has been great interest in an identification of the highly noxious gases which appear in the form of a bluish haze. The first attempt to collect samples of such gases was apparently made at Hekla in 1846, the summer after it erupted. The result was disappointing because a chemical analysis of the samples revealed mainly atmosphere, carbon dioxide and water. The first successful attempts to collect gases from a volcanic crater were made on Hawaii, and some measure of success has also been achieved along the same lines at Nyiragongo in Africa and on Stromboli. After the Hekla eruption of 1947–48 and the Askja eruption of 1961 some attempts at gas collection from lava fissures and steamholes were made, but the samples again turned out to consist largely of atmosphere mixed with carbon dioxide. In 1964 many attempts were made at collecting volcanic gases on Surtsey, both from red-hot lava fissures where the temperature was 800 °C and from the main crater where the temperature was about 1200 °C. At first many of the attempts were unsuccessful. Some of the instruments could not withstand the temperature, but others simply dissolved in acid vapours. Finally, however, a place in the Surtsey lava was discovered which had some unique characteristics that were favourable for the collection of gas samples. Then the lava flowed from the crater through a big subterranean channel, but in one place there was a narrow slit in the roof of the channel through which gas streamed out at great speed. As the gas escaped from the slit it caught fire so that a narrow flame stood out of the hole in the lava. An attempt was made to measure the temperature by means of an electric thermometer housed in an iron cylinder, but the flame melted the iron in an instant and ruined the thermometer. Thus the temperature must have exceeded 1300 °C. Here some gas samples could be captured and fed to collection containers through a stainless steel pipe by means of its own pressure. A chemical analysis of this gas showed that it was entirely uncontaminated by the atmosphere, and this is possibly the best sample that has been retrieved from a volcanic area up to now. Water vapour proved to be 80% of its content, and apart from water the gases consisted of sulphur dioxide (SO_2), hydrogen and carbon dioxide with small amounts of carbon monoxide, nitrogen and argon in addition to some hydrogen chloride and sulphuric vapour.

Constantly chemical research has been made into the nature of the loose volcanic material and the lava produced by the Surtsey eruption. As might be expected there is no chemical difference between the tephra and the lava. Rapid cooling of the magma causes the formation of tephra, but slow cooling results in the formation of lava. These studies

⇨

In the top of the map volcanic areas that have been active since the last ice-age are indicated by shading, some of the volcanoes being indicated by name. Most of the volcanic areas are within a wide belt lying askew across the centre of the country from south-west to northeast. Outside this belt, however, are Snæfellsnes and Öræfajökull. All this volcanic area is approximately 35.000 km². The lower map shows the location of Surtsey in relation to the Vestmannaeyjar and the mainland. On the Heimaey is shown the old volcano Helgafell, and the new one Eldfell, which erupted in 1973.

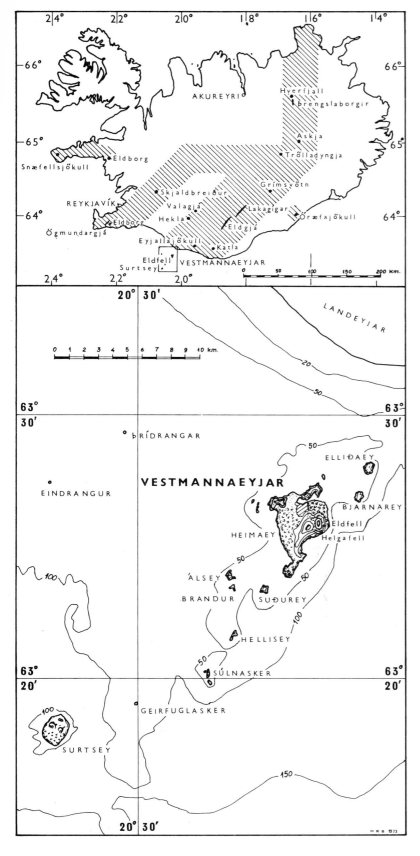

have also revealed that the Surtsey lava is totally different from those of Askja and Hekla. It is more similar to volcanic materials from Katla and Eldgjá, but there are differences, however. Volcanologists have concluded on the basis of this evidence that Surtsey does not derive from a magma reservoir which is shared by any volcano on the mainland of Iceland.

It was mentioned above (see p. 30) that a submarine eruption has some similarities to a subglacial one, and the Surtsey eruption has shown without any doubt that it is water coming from outside which causes the magma to disintegrate with the resulting tephra being flung high up in the air. On page 124 it is mentioned that the table mountain Herðubreið was formed by a volcanic eruption underneath an ice-age glacier. If the sea around Surtsey disappeared, we would see a mountain that looked very much like table mountains, but in time the volcanic tephra turns to palagonite tuff, although it is not known how long such a development takes. Resting on the tuff base of Surtsey is the lava shield produced by the effusive eruption. According to the table mountain theory the chain of events leading to the formation of both Surtsey in the sea and Herðubreið and other table mountains on land is as follows: The first magma flowing out of a volcanic fissure in the sea or underneath a thick glacier turns to pillow lava, which has a vitreous crust over a crystallized rock interior. The surrounding water or sea absorbs all vapours and other combustible materials so that there are no explosions owing to the overwhelming pressure of the water. So far no eruption has found its way to the surface of the glacier or the sea. The glacier melts from underneath and a pile of pillow lava rises into an ice dome full of water (or from the sea-bed in the case of a submarine eruption). Finally, the pressure from above can no longer withstand the internal pressure of the volcanic gases, and the result is a violent explosive eruption. Then the issuing magma changes to cinders or tephra owing to rapid cooling. The explosive eruption piles up tephra on top of the pillow lava, a raw material for palagonite tuff. If the explosive eruption lasts long enough for the volcanic material to break through the surface of the ice cap (or the sea), there will be a continuous hot ash eruption, followed by an effusive eruption with a lava flow if the tephra succeeds in preventing water (or seawater) from reaching the magma on its way to the surface. So far it has not been possible to determine whether there is pillow lava under the Surtsey socle, and it would in any case be very deep down.

Geophysical studies of the Surtsey eruption have been concerned with various of its aspects. The emission speed of the volcanic material from the Surtsey vents was measured and found to be 150-200 m/sec and the eruption column reached a height of 9 km when the conditions in the upper layers of the atmosphere were favourable. Lightning flashes appeared in the eruption column during the first few months of the eruption. Many aspects of its influence on the surrounding sea were studied. If all the energy generated by the eruption had been spent on heating up the ocean, it would have raised the temperature of one km^3 of sea by 2° C. As the depth of the sea is only 130 m near Surtsey we might have expected a measurable increase in temperature over a large area, but that was not the case. The tephra apparently acted as an effective insulator between the magma and the sea with the result that the eruption released much more heat to the atmosphere than to the sea. Geomagnetic measurements were made both from the air and on the island itself. It was found that the magnetic field of the lava is highly anomalous, whereas the field of the tephra areas is very homogeneous, the tephra being about 100 times less magnetized than the lava. Special seismographic measurements were made on the occasion of the Surtsey eruption in addition to measurements made by permanent seismographs located on the mainland. In general the earth is quiet during a lava-producing eruption, but earthquakes are more liable to occur during explosive eruptions. The tremors were sharpest when the

eruption was moving from one vent to another on Surtsey itself, or from Surtsey to Syrtlingur. The temperature of the lava in the crater was measured by inserting a 10 m long chromel-almud thermocouple into the magma and keeping it there until the voltmeter ceased to rise. This took no more than a minute, but during this time so much lava had accumulated on the thermocouple that two men had difficulties in retrieving it. Two measurements were made in this way, but it was found inadvisable to carry them out more often owing to the risks involved. The measurements recorded the temperatures of 1150 °C and 1160 °C respectively, so it is thought likely that the temperature of the magma flowing to the crater was 1150–1200 °C.

It is not possible to give a more detailed account here of the research carried out on Surtsey, in which a number of scientists are still actively engaged. Many tasks still need to be done even though the eruption has ceased. The genesis of this fire island has been told to some extent here in words and pictures, but its formative history lies largely in the future, which will reveal Nature's pleasure of dressing it with vegetation and adorning it with animals. In Surtsey Nature has presented us with a research station to enable us to increase our knowledge of various factors of geological history and of life on earth.

There have been lava eruptions in every century of Icelandic history so they are well-known to all Icelanders. In many parts of the country there are relatively young and bare lava fields which show quite clearly where the flow came from and how it behaved, e.g. whether it was viscous and slow-moving or thin as a soup and fast-moving. There are lava channels, rough black lava and undulating lava fields, lava craters and explosive craters of countless dimensions and types, upright lava rocks and caves. The variety of lava formations is virtually infinite, and a close examination may reveal many aspects of their origin. To witness a flow of glowing lava is a unique experience as it presents a live demonstration of the creation of the many different

⇨

One of the most remarkable phenomena of the Surtsey eruption was the red-hot lava flowing into the sea. Sometimes the lava surged forward inside a solidified lava crust which now and then burst open with the result that the sea came in direct contact with the molten lava. Then there were sometimes great explosions which ejected lava splashes high up in the air.

There is still considerable heat under the Surtsey lava even though the surface is cold enough for snow to stay on the ground. This picture of Surtsey with the Vestmannaeyjar in the background was taken on February 8th 1970. The picture is certainly symbolic for the whole of Iceland, a land of ice and fire. Underneath snow and glacial firn there is fire. Great are the contrasts of Icelandic nature.

160

lava formations. After an effusive eruption started on Surtsey the volcanic activity behaved very much like an eruption on land. One point, however, made this fire island extraordinary: It was the interplay of the forces of fire and those of the sea. The variety of this spectacle made it fascinating to watch for long periods at a time. When the lava flow was in spate, a wide lava stream might pour in the sea and it could be seen progressing along the sea-bed for long distances. When the flow was less forceful, it rolled into the sea inside fragile pockets of solidified lava, and from time to time small rifts opened and glowing lava rivulets plunged into the sea-surge. It was interesting to watch how the lava streams sometimes turned a sharp corner to the side when they approached the sea as if they shrank from contact with the water. This happened quite frequently when the flow was not particularly fast-moving. Then the cooling was quickest in the part of the lava stream which was closest to the sea with the result that a dam might be piled up along the sea-shore. Sometimes, however, openings developed in this dam, through which the lava found its way to the sea. Then big jets of steam rose from the sea as the red-hot lava tongue disintegrated to the glassy cinders which make up the sandy beaches of Surtsey. The lava could be crossed on foot, even if it was considerably hot, because an insulating crust soon developed. Often, however, it floated on red-hot liquid lava underneath. In many places, however, it was impossible to stand still on this lava crust, and rucksacks or other luggage could not be put down without a risk of damage. Before Pálsbær, the hut of the Surtsey Research Society, was built, visitors to Surtsey stayed in tents. The conditions radically changed with the advent of Pálsbær, both in respect of sleeping-quarters and storage facilities for instruments, cameras etc. When a weary visitor to Surtsey lies down to sleep at night after a tour of this extraordinary island, he cannot help marvelling at the enormity of the natural forces which created it. In the October of 1963 there was no land here. Now we have a sandy beach strewn with sea-worn boulders which even the most competent geologists might think were many hundreds of years old if they did not know their origin. Here we have sea-cliffs which look like ancient rock-formations. Eruptions have taken place off the Icelandic coast before in historical time, and in the annals for 1211 it is stated that Sörli Kolsson discovered 'The New Fire Islands', whereas the old ones, which had been there from time immemorial, had disappeared. Thus it is indicated that some islands emerged off the Icelandic coast in 1211, and at the same time some other islands vanished. The name of those which disappeared indicates that they, too, were of volcanic origin. No doubt this volcanism occurred on the submarine ridge which extends south-westwards from the Reykjanes Peninsula along the whole length of the Atlantic towards the Antarctic and northwards from Iceland to Jan Mayen. Volcanic eruptions off the Reykjanes Peninsula are referred to in annals for the years 1226, 1231, 1238, 1240, 1422, and 1583. Finally, there is a reliable source on, and an eye-witness account of, an eruption off the Reykjanes Peninsula in the spring of 1783. A ship arrived on the scene when an island had emerged from the sea. The captain made a sketch of the island which looks very much like Surtsey as it was in the initial phase of the eruption. This island was called Nýey ('New Island'), but when it was to be dedicated to King Christian VII with a stone bearing his initials and the appropriate date, the island had been engulfed by the sea again. But Surtsey is definitely there to stay. The lava still emits some heat, but in winter it is occasionally covered with snow. Nobody who now flies over the Vestmannaeyjar archipelago is able to discern that one of these islands was born in fire only a few years ago.

fire in Hekla

An eruption started in Mt Hekla about 9.30 p.m. on May 5th 1970. The last major eruption of Hekla took place in 1947–48. Shorter intervals between Hekla eruptions have occurred, but this eruption took scientists and laymen alike entirely unawares. It was not until 20.48 that same night that earth tremors were registered on seismographs in Reykjavik, the biggest tremor occurring at 21.40 As soon as the eruption started a black column of smoke rose from the mountain and in neighbouring districts red flames of fire were seen to reach a long way up the eruption column, which reached a height of almost 15 km. The wind was blowing from the south-east when the eruption began, directing the ashes in a north-westerly direction. Near the Burfell power station lumps of pumice as big as a man's fist rained down together with the ashes. As usual, the tephra-fall was most intense during the first few hours, the tephra layer being up to 17 cm. thick in the centre of the tephra-fall area. To judge by the fire columns that were seen it soon became clear that the Hekla ridge had not opened lengthwise as happens when there are major eruptions in the volcano proper. Instead volcanic fissures had opened in three separate places. Two of them were in the upper parts of the mountain slopes,

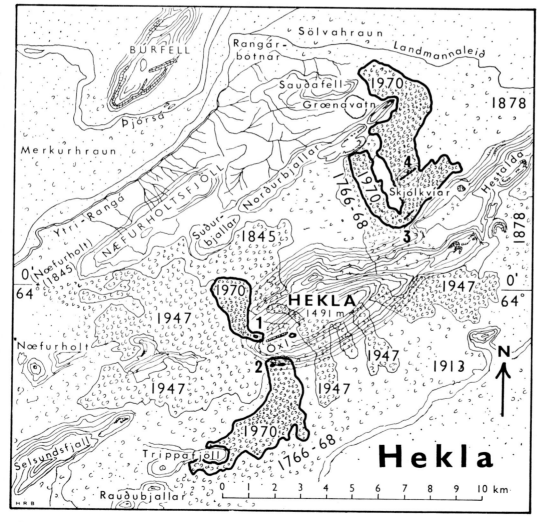

Hekla and its immediate vicinity. The three volcanic areas which became active on May 5th 1970 are marked 1, 2, and 3. Area 1 to the north of Hekla's Shoulder Crater produced the least lava, the eruption there lasting only a short period. Much more lava flowed from the crater row on the south side of Hekla (2), reaching as far as Trippafjöll. The Skjólkvíar eruption to the north-west of Hekla proper (3) was of the longest duration. The resulting lava inundated the Hringlandahraun lava of 1766–68. New active craters opened up in a sand hill in the Skjólkvíar area on May 20th, from which lava flowed all the way past Sauðafell above Rangárbotnar. A few older lava areas are indicated on the map, e.g. Næfurholtshraun of 1845, when the farm Næfurholt was moved because of the lava flow.

The Skjólvíkar eruption (marked 3 on the map) in the evening of May 7th 1970. The eruption constantly moved from one place to another along the volcanic fissure. A small fire hole which opened in a closed part of the fissure sometimes developed into the most active vent in half an hour. At the same time the whole area reverberated with bangs and rumble while red-hot lava splashes were hurled hundreds of metres up in the air and then fell back, still glowing, on the crater rims where they flattened out and solidified.

163

An eruption in the second lot of Skjól-kvíar craters (marked 4 on the map on p. 162) in the evening of May 24th 1970. A view from Norðurbjallar over the new lava flows and the crater rows in the Skjólkvíar sand hill. The north-east side of Hekla is in the background.

The lava edge to the north-east of Norðurbjallar in the late evening of May 24th 1970. Motor vehicles could be driven right up to the edge of the lava, but their drivers had to take care not to leave them too close to the lava since its advance was more rapid than many realized. In one night the motor car tracks seen in the picture were engulfed by the firy lava.

The advance of the lava edge in Skjólkvíar is accompanied by some grinding noise and clatter as the insulating hardened crust on top of the red-hot lava flow presses forward and disintegrates. Where the lava advances at its highest speed, the molten basalt lava is easily visible.

Many a fascinated spectator watched in awe the advancing lava stream which in a few days inundated twenty km² of land, sand, old lava and grassland alike.

165

one on the north side, marked 1 on the map on page 162, and the other, marked 2, on the south side. The third fissure, which opened at the same time as the other two, was not in Hekla proper, but to the north-east of the mountain near old craters in Skjólkvíar (3). At the beginning the eruption from the fissure in the south-side of Hekla was by far the most forceful, the lava masses being ejected to a height of approximately 750 m from a row of craters. From it a continuous red-hot lava stream of more or less uniform width flowed down the slopes of Hekla in the direction of Trippafjöll. The eruption in, and the lava flow from, the fissure in the north side of Hekla was less intense than in the other areas, whereas the Skjólkvíar eruption soon increased in intensity. There the lava flow engulfed a snow-covered area, melting the snow as it advanced. Ice and fire were in a very real contact here, causing dark-brown streams of water to rush down newly-formed river beds. In the first four days of the eruption the new lava spread over an area of about 19 km². – As the eruption started at the beginning of the lambing-season and all vegetation was just entering a sensitive revival period after the winter, some livestock were killed by fluor poisoning in the areas that were worst hit by the tephra fall both in the South and North of Iceland, even though in many places sheep and cattle were kept inside under medical attention or transferred to unpolluted areas. An analysis of the eruption material revealed the same chemical structure as that of the lava produced in the 1947–48 eruption of Hekla (andesite). The crater, marked 1 on the map on page 162, on the north side of the Hekla ridge erupted for only a short time, being the highest area that was active during this eruption. There the lava-flow had completely ceased by the evening of May 6th. The eruption in the south side of the mountain (2) continued a little longer where a large volume of lava flowed all the way to the Trippafjöll, covering an old lava dating from the 1766–68 eruption. In this area no lava was seen to flow after May 9th, but there was red-hot lava in the crater and a lot of smoke much longer. Of the three volcanic areas which became active on May 5th the third (marked 3 on the map) erupted longest, being on the lowest level. It was fascinating to watch the fire columns constantly shifting from one end of the fissure to the other. Heavy thuds and rumbling noise accompanied the explosions which ejected the red-hot lava masses as high as 500 m up in the air. Later crater cones were built up by the solidified ejecta, confining the eruption to a few vents that were at first all active simultaneously. By May 12th, however, only one of the vents remained active. The lava from these vents flowed mainly in two directions, i.e. across the Hringlanda lava of 1766–68 in the direction of Norðurbjallar and downwards by the Hestalda mountain ridge. The lava surrounded a big sand hill in Skjólkvíar. In the afternoon of May 20th the lava ceased to flow from the last active vent in this area, but about the same time a new volcanic fissure, lying in the direction NE to SW, opened up about one kilometre further to the north, i.e. on the north side of the sand hill mentioned above. In the beginning there were about 20 eruption columns in a fissure that was about one km long, but they soon decreased in number. A voluminous stream of lava flowed from this volcanic area (marked 4 on the map on page 162). The lava flowed in a northerly direction past the end of Sauðafell. Motor cars could be driven right up to the craters and the edge of the lava, so hardly ever has an active volcanic area in Iceland been more easily accessible than this one. The lava flowing down the crater walls travelled at a speed of 3–5 m a second and the edge of the lava 4 km away from the crater sometimes advanced 5–10 metres an hour. Some vegetation was engulfed by the lava and a few hours' old motor car tracks disappeared for ever under the advancing lava wall. In front of it there were silent spectators, retreating as they watched this stupendous turmoil of the land which 11 centuries ago received the name of Iceland but which might just as well have been called 'Fireland'.

An overnight stay near the Skjólkvíar craters (marked 4 on the map on p. 162) was an unforgettable experience. Many of the sand hill craters were active simultaneously, presenting a veritable 'candlestick of craters'. This area was easily accessible by motorized transport and therefore there was a ceaseless flow of tourists to these craters. To the right there is a lava rivulet issuing from the vents.

postscript

When I have now reached the final stage of this work there are many memories to cherish and acknowledgements to make. The oldest picture was taken on Drangajökull in 1938, but the latest one was taken during the Hekla eruption of 1970. Yet, a great majority of the pictures have been taken during the last 8 years. On my travels I have had many good companions. I will always remember the enjoyable time I spent with my fellow-members of the Iceland Glaciological Society and the Surtsey Research Society. In connection with many other tours I would in particular mention the pleasant company of Systems Engineer Óttar Kjartansson. Photography of Icelandic nature demands both time and patience. A painstaking enthusiast for photography may certainly slow down fellow-travellers who wish to cover a good distance in one day. Therefore I very much appreciate the understanding that I have been shown by all my fellow-travellers when a special opportunity of photographic work was at stake. Naturally a photographer is sometimes better off if he travels alone, but it is not always advisible to do so in the highlands of Iceland and least of all on glaciers.

The purpose of this book is to illustrate in words and pictures the contrasts of Icelandic nature, ice and fire. Its first part deals with sea ice and glaciers, and it concludes with an account of hot springs and volcanic eruptions. It is not a general description of Iceland and her people. That is a subject I dealt with to some extent in my book 'Iceland'. Both ice and fire are, indeed, very much intertwined with the history of the Icelandic people right from the time of the settlement down to the present days as I have attempted to explain in this book. These opposing forces of nature have not always given the Icelandic people a kid-glove treatment. All the same the Icelandic people have learned to appreciate and evaluate these forces as inseparable parts of Icelandic nature. This book is also intended to call attention to the values that are inherent in the magnificent beauty of virgin nature. This is principally the role of the photographs. But to enable the reader to acquire a deeper understanding of the material I have prepared a text, containing some information on the natural phenomena dealt with, and added some maps and drawings to explain certain aspects of it in greater detail.

In my discussion of any specialized subject I have, of course, drawn on various sources. Many of the authors and their collaborators are personally known to me from my travels to Vatnajökull and Surtsey. Two men sharing a tent in a driving tephra-fall on Surtsey or in a sleety snowstorm on Vatnajökull are bound to become thoroughly acquainted. To me such an acquaintance has been an invaluable source of information and pleasure. Their keen interest in their research projects has been catching. Every opportunity has been taken to explore and study at first hand any natural phenomena which had not been quite clear. It is the nature of the child and the scientist alike to ask 'why' and to expect an answer.

A detailed bibliography follows. Books and papers are arranged in an alphabetical order of their authors, i.e. the patronymic names of Icelandic authors and the surnames of others in the usual way. In the case of collective authorship, the name of the work decides the order in which it is listed. Figures after the name of a paper or a book denote page numbers in that work, but figures after the sign □ refer to pages in this book where references are made to a particular source or where some relevant information touches the subject in question. Where a particular page is not referred to, the source is usually one which might be expected to be useful for the reader regarding further general information on the subject-matter of this book.

I owe thanks to the National Library of Iceland for permission to photograph the map of Iceland by Bishop Guðbrandur Þorláksson, and to Librarian Haraldur Sigurðsson for assistance and useful information on the map. Thanks are also due to Professor Jón Helgason of the Arnemagnean Library in Copenhagen for permission to photograph a page of Landnámabók ('Book of Settlements') and for other kind assistance. For translation of Latin texts I owe thanks to Dr. Jakob Benediktsson.

Oceanographer Dr. Unnsteinn Stefánsson assisted me in drawing the ocean-current and sea-ice charts and read through several sections including those on sea ice, drift ice and the sea ice and Iceland. Pétur Sigurðsson, Director of the Icelandic Coast Guard, lent a chart of sea-ice off Iceland. Ágúst Böðvarsson, Head of the Icelandic Geodetic Survey, kindly permitted me to make use of aerial survey photographs of Vatnajökull, Surtsey and Hekla for the drawing of my maps of these places for this book. Gunnar Bergsteinsson, Head of the Icelandic Hydrographic Survey, made available charts for drawing up the map of Surtsey in relation to Vestmannaeyjar. Hlynur Sigtryggsson, Director of the Icelandic Meteorological Office, permitted the printing on page 16 of pictures which show the distribution of sea ice off Iceland. Historian Björn Þorsteinsson checked historical references, and Óttar Kjartansson read the manuscript from the point of view of the Iceland traveller. Advertising artist Torfi Jónsson gave some advice on the layout of the book. The authors of the sources on which I have drawn have been most kind in giving me material information. I wish to extend my gratitude to all these people for their assistance.

Last but not least I wish to thank Geologist Dr. Sigurður Þórarinsson. He has given invaluable assistance by reading all the manuscript and offering his advice on several points of substance.

Hjálmar R Bárðarson

bibliography

Books and papers are arranged in an alphabetical order of their authors. Icelandic authors are referred to by their patronymic names and others by their surnames. In the case of collective authorship the name of the work decides the order in which it is listed.

Armstrong, T., Roberts B., & Swithinbank Ch., 1966. Illustrated Glossary of Snow and Ice. Cambridge.

Árnason, Bragi. 1968. Tvívetni í grunnvatni og jöklum á Íslandi (Deuterium in Ground Water and Glaciers in Iceland). Jökull, 337–349. Reykjavík. □ 58, 59.

Áskelsson, Jóhannes. 1936. On the Last Eruption in Vatnajökull. Reykjavík. □ 54–56.

Bárðarson (Bardarson), Guðmundur G., 1934. Islands Gletscher. Reykjavík. □ 24–40.

Bárðarson (Bardarson), Hjálmar R. 1965. Ísland, Iceland, Islande. Reykjavík.

– 1966. Jökulskinna, gestabók á Hrolleifsborg í Drangajökli (The Visitors' Book Jökulskinna at Hrolleifsborg, Drangajökull). Jökull 219–225. Reykjavík. □ 24–28.

– 1969. Ísing skipa. Hafísinn 439–469. Reykjavík. □ 92.

– 1969. Icing of Ships. Jökull, 107–120. Reykjavík □ 92.

Benediktsson, Jakob. 1968. Gerðir Landnámabókar. Reykjavík. □ 8.

Björnsson, Sigurður. 1962. Undirvarp. (With summary. Jökull 44–45. Reykjavík. □ 80, 82.

Drift Ice and Climate. Symposium held in Reykjavik from 27th January to 7th February 1969. Dedicated to the Memory of Jón Eythorsson. Abridged versions of most of the 30 lectures presented were published in English in the 1969 issue of Jökull, Journal of the Iceland Glaciological Society, Reykjavík. In the book Hafísinn (The Drift Ice), Reykjavík 1969, the lectures were published in Icelandic.

Dyson, James L., 1963. The World of Ice. London. □ 4–7.

Einarsson, Trausti. 1948. Bergmyndunarsaga Vestmannaeyja. Árbók Ferðafélags Íslands: 131–157. Reykjavík. □ 124.

– 1961. Upphaf Íslands og blágrýtismyndunin. Náttúra Íslands, 11–29. Reykjavík. □ 86.

– 1961. Geysir og Geysisgos. Árbók Ferðafélags Íslands, 73–77. Reykjavík. □ 113, 114.

Einarsson, Þorleifur. 1965. Gosið í Surtsey í máli og myndum. Reykjavík.

Eyþórsson (Eythorsson), Jón. 1931. On the Present Position of the Glaciers in Iceland. Reykjavik. □ 24–51.

– 1960. Vatnajökull. Reykjavík. □ 47–51.

– 1961. Verðurfar. Náttúra Íslands, 141–154. Reykjavík. □ 98.

– 1961. Jöklar. Náttúra Íslands, 155–168. Reykjavík. □ 24, 26, 27, 29–40, 47–51.

– 1962. Norður yfir Vatnajökul 1875, W. L. Watts, Reykjavík. □ 51, 60.

Friðriksson (Fridriksson), Sturla. 1967. Life and its Development on the Volcanic Island Surtsey. Proceedings of the Surtsey Research Conference, Reykjavik 1967. 7–19. □ 155–156.

Groen, P., 1967. The Waters of the Sea. London. □ 6–7.

Hafís við Ísland (collective authorship), 1968. Reykjavík.

Hafísinn (collective authorship), 1969. Reykjavík.

Jóhansson, Guðgeir. 1919. Kötlugosið 1918. Reykjavík. □ 40.

Jónsson, Jón. 1961. Jarðhiti. Náttúra Íslands. 95–119. Reykjavík. □ 108.

Jónsson, Ólafur. 1945. Ódáðahraun I, II, III. – Kverkfjöll (I), 122–145. □ 101, 103.

– 1946. Frá Kröflu. Náttúrufræðingurinn, 152–157. Reykjavík. □ 108.

– 1962. Dyngjufjöll og Askja. Akureyri.

Jökull, ársrit Jöklarannsóknafélags Íslands. 1951–1970. (Journal of Iceland Glaciological Society). Reykjavík.

Kjartansson, Guðmundur. 1943. Jarðsaga, Árnesingasaga I: 1–250. Reykjavík. □ 124.

– 1945. Hekla. Árbók Ferðafélags Íslands. Reykjavík. □ 119, 126.

– 1947. Þættir af Heklugosinu. Náttúrufræðingurinn. 49–56, 180–184. Reykjavík. □ 119, 126.

– 1948. Þættir af Heklugosinu. Náttúrufræðingurinn. 9–22, Reykjavík. □ 119.

– 1966. Stapakenningin og Surtsey. Náttúrufræðingurinn, 1–34. (Summary: A Comparison of Tablemountains in Iceland and the Volcanic Island of Surtsey off the South Coast of Iceland). Reykjavík. □ 124, 157–158.

Kristjánsson, Andrés. 1963. Geysir á Bárðarbungu. Reykjavík. □ 51.

Landnámabók. Manuscript: Sturlubók, AM. 107 fol. Copy by Jón Erlendsson, 17th century. □ 8, 13.

Lárusson, Magnús Már. 1969. Hafís á fyrri öldum. Hafísinn. Reykjavík. 306–312. □ 13, 14.

Nielsen, Niels. 1938. Vatnajökull. Barátta elds og ísa. Reykjavík.

Nörlund, N. E., 1944 Islands Kortlægning. Guðbrandur Thorlaksson, 28–30. København. □ 2.

Pálsson, Sveinn (1762–1840). Ferðabók 1791–1797. Reykjavík 1945. □ 27–29, 70, 74, 77.

Pounder, Elton R., 1965. The Physics of Ice. London. □ 4, 5.

Rist, Sigurjón. 1951. Grænalón. Náttúrufræðingurinn. Reykjavík. 184–186. □ 82.

– 1956. Íslenzk vötn (Icelandic Fresh Waters). Reykjavík. □ 98.

– 1961. Vötn. Náttúra Íslands, 169–192. Reykjavík. □ 98.

Schultz. Gwen. 1963. Glaciers and the Ice Age. New York.

Sigtryggsson, Hlynur. 1969. Yfirlit um hafís í grennd við Ísland. Hafísinn 80–94. Reykjavík. □ 16–20.

Sigurðsson (Sigurdsson, Vigfús (Grænlandsfari). 1948. Um þvert Grænland með Kapt. J. P. Koch, 1912–1913. 7–20. Reykjavík. □ 51.

Sigurgeirsson, Þorbjörn. 1966. Jarðeðlisfræðirannsóknir í sambandi við Surtseyjargosið (Geophysical Research in connection with the Volcanic Eruption at Surtsey). Náttúrufræðingurinn, 188–210.

Reykjavík. □ 158.

Sigvaldason, Guðmundur E. 1965. Um rannsóknir á gosefnum frá Surtsey (Geochemical Studies on Surtsey). Náttúrufræðingurinn. 181–188. Reykjavík. □ 156, 158.

Skaptason, Jóhann. 1959. Árbók Ferðafélags Íslands. Barðastrandarsýsla. 95–96. Reykjavík. □ 8.

Skýrslur um Skaptárgosin 1783. Safn til sögu Íslands VI. Kaupmannahöfn and Reykjavík, 1907–1915. □ 128.

Stefánsson, Unnsteinn. 1961, Hafið. Reykjavík.

Surtsey Research Progress Report. II, 1966; III. 1967; IV 1968. Reykjavík.

Surtsey Research Conference 1967. Reykjavík.

Theodórsson, Páll. 1968. Þrívetni í grunnvatni og jöklum á Íslandi (Tritium in Ground Water and Glaciers in Iceland). Jökull. 350–358. □ 58, 59.

Thoroddsen, Þorvaldur. 1913–1915 & 1959: Ferðabók I, II, III & IV. Köbenhavn & Reykjavík. □ 80.

– 1916–1917. Árferði á Íslandi í þúsund ár. Köbenhavn □ 13–20.

Vatnasvið Íslands (Iceland's Drainage Net). 1969. Reykjavík. □ 98.

Verne, Jules. 1864. Voyage au centre de la terre. Paris. Leyndardómar Snæfellsjökuls, för í iður jarðar. Translation into Icelandic by Bjarni Guðmundsson. Reykjavík 1944. □ 44.

Vídalin, Þórður Þorkelsson. c. 1690–1695: Jöklarit. Reykjavík, 1965.

Vilmundarson, Þórhallur. 1969. Heimildir um hafís á síðari öldum. Hafísinn. Reykjavík. 313–332. □ 13, 14.

Watts, W. L., 1875. Across the Vatnajökull, or Scenes in Iceland. Norður yfir Vatnajökull 1875. Reykjavík 1962. □ 48, 51, 60.

Þórarinsson (Thorarinsson), Sigurður. 1956: The Thousand Years' Struggle against Ice and Fire. Reykjavík. □ 24, 26, 27, 29–40.

– 1950. Jökulhlaup og eldgos á jökulvatnasvæði Jökulsár á Fjöllum. (Glacier Outbursts in the River Jökulsá á Fjöllum). Náttúrufræðingurinn. 113–133. Reykjavík. □ 103.

– 1960. Glaciological Knowledge in Iceland before 1800. Jökull, 1–17. Reykjavík. □ 24, 26, 27.

– 1961. Eldstöðvar og hraun. Náttúra Íslands. 65–93. Reykjavík. □ 74, 77, 107, 117, 118, 119.

– 1962. On the Age of the Terminal Moraines of Brúarjökull and Hálsajökull. Jökull, 67–75. Reykjavík. □ 49.

– 1962. Sudden Advance of Vatnajökull Outlet Glaciers 1930–1964. Jökull, 76–89. Reykjavík. □ 49.

– 1963. Eldur í Öskju. (Askja on Fire). Reykjavík.

– 1964. Surtsey. Eyjan nýja í Atlantshafi. Reykjavík.

– 1965. Surtsey: Island Born of Fire. 713–726. National Geographic. Washington.

– 1965. Sitt af hverju um Surtseyjargosið (Some Facts about the Surtsey Eruption). Náttúrufræðingurinn 153–181. Reykjavík. □ 130–138.

– 1967. The Eruption of Hekla 1947–1948. I. The Eruption of Hekla in Historical Times. A Tephrachronological Study. Reykjavík. □ 119, 126.

– 1967. Skaftáreldar og Lakagígar. (Summary: The Lakagígar Eruption of 1783 and the Lakagígar Crater Row). Náttúrufræðingurinn, 27–57. Reykjavík. □ 128.

– 1968. Síðustu þættir Eyjaelda. (The Last Phases of the Surtsey Eruption). Náttúrufræðingurinn, 113–135. Reykjavík. □ 142, 151.

index